Praise for The [illegible]

'Not surprisingly Emma has delivered the best book on presentation skills I have ever come across. Having experienced her training course first hand, and immediate success in selling consulting work shortly after, I can say with full confidence that she is exceptional at what she does. *The Presentation Book* provides compelling, practical and pithy advice that is easy to take in and apply. It will be my go to resource for presentations and communications in general from now on.'

Robert Freese, Director, Talent and Organisation Development, First Data Corporation

The Presentation Book exemplifies what Emma does best – communicate the complex clearly, concisely and with great consideration for her audience. This is a truly insightful and practical book that will undoubtedly inspire many in the delivery of more impactful and influential communications.'

Johanna Fullerton, Business Psychologist and Director, SEVEN, Psychology at Work

'Finally, there is a book that can guide the most inexperienced presenter to deliver a top class presentation, as well as help the more experienced presenter figure out how to get better results from the presentations they deliver. Full of simple yet incredibly effective models that will help shape and create powerful presentations, as well as practical advice on delivering compelling messages that connect with the audience and create the right impression.'

Mary O'Reilly, Senior Manager, Talent, Development and Learning, Deloitte & Touche

The Presentation Book is a really practical guide for anyone who is involved in presenting. It is very engaging and an easy read with lots of useful real-life examples and templates for guidance. This book will support those new to presenting through the preparation process and to encourage the more experienced presenter to improve and refine their approach.'

Elaine McGleenan, Director, Learning and Organisational Development, KPMG

The Presentation Book

The Presentation Book

How to create it, shape it and deliver it!

Emma Ledden

PEARSON

Harlow, England • London • New York • Boston • San Francisco • Toronto • Sydney
Auckland • Singapore • Hong Kong • Tokyo • Seoul • Taipei • New Delhi
Cape Town • São Paulo • Mexico City • Madrid • Amsterdam • Munich • Paris • Milan

PEARSON EDUCATION LIMITED
Edinburgh Gate
Harlow CM20 2JE
United Kingdom
Tel: +44 (0)1279 623623
Web: www.pearson.com/uk

First published 2013 (print and electronic)

ISBN: 978-1-292-00258-3 (print)
978-1-292-00287-3 (PDF)
978-1-292-00286-6 (ePub)
978-1-292-00822-6 (eText)

British Library Cataloguing-in-Publication Data
A catalogue record for the print edition is available from the British Library

Library of Congress Cataloging-in-Publication Data
Ledden, Emma.
The presentation book : how to create it, shape it and deliver it! / Emma Ledden.
pages cm
Includes index.
ISBN 978-1-292-00258-3 -- ISBN 978-1-292-00287-3 (PDF) -- ISBN 978-1-292-00286-6 (ePub) -- ISBN 978-1-292-00822-6 (eText)
1. Business presentations. I. Title.
HF5718.22.L424 2013
658.4'52--dc23
2013027809

10 9 8 7 6 5 4 3 2 1
17 16 15 14 13

Text design by Design Deluxe
Cover design by redeyoffdesign, cover images © L_amica/Shutterstock.com and phipatbig/Shutterstock.com

Print edition typeset in 9.5/13pt Mundo Sans Std by 3
Printed in Great Britain by Henry Ling Ltd, at the Dorset Press, Dorchester, Dorset

NOTE THAT ANY PAGE CROSS REFERENCES REFER TO THE PRINT EDITION

The Presentation Book promise

This book will give you a three-step approach to filter all your data through to transform it into a clear, sharp and influential presentation.

This book will give you the knowledge and framework to engage an audience and present in a way that will get results.

This book will give you the ability to have an audience hang on your every word.

CONTENTS

ABOUT THE AUTHOR

In her 35 years, Emma Ledden has done it all – MTV VJ, BBC TV presenter, radio host, businesswoman, speaker and author.

Emma began her career presenting for Ireland's national broadcaster producing and presenting her own slot for two and a half years. Following this, Emma was chosen from over 2,000 hopefuls to become a VJ for MTV UK. This involved being in front of a television camera five days a week. Here, she presented *The Dancefloor Chart Show*, *Select*, *Weekend Edition* and *MTV News*. Within six months Emma had landed another very high-profile television position. She was chosen to present the BBC's flagship programme *Live and Kicking*.

During this time Emma fronted major ad campaigns including Pepsi and Lee Jeans as well as gracing the front covers and pages of international magazines including *Maxim*, *Ministry*, *Loaded*, *Heat*, *FHM* and *Company*. Emma has interviewed some of the world's biggest stars including Posh and Becks, Kylie Minogue, Robbie Williams, The Spice Girls, Justin Timberlake, Gwen Stefani, The Rock, Britney, Take That and Beyoncé.

Emma also worked in radio for a number of years. Initially she worked on a weekend magazine programme and then progressed to producing and presenting a breakfast programme. Emma still contributes to the media and is a regular panellist and presenter on radio and television.

In 2007 Emma set up her own company and developed *The Presentation Book* approach under the business brand of Presenting To Sell: www.presentingtosell.com

Today, Emma is a leading international presentation skills consultant. She works with companies such as Deloitte, Matheson, KPMG, Ericsson and many other private and public organisations as well as individual business leaders to help them win both credibility and business.

ACKNOWLEDGEMENTS

I would like to dedicate this book to my mum (aka little Sue). Mum, you are the most beautiful, original and fun person I know. I definitely got the best one. Thank you for everything.

I would also like to thank the rest of my family for all their love and support over the years; to my friends for always making me laugh – I am so lucky to have you; to Geraldine Sweeney for your support and Edward Fidgeon-Kavanagh, it was a pleasure to work with you; to Pearson for saying 'yes'; for Rachael Stock and Eloise Cook for turning a first draft into a manuscript; to the Pearson creative team for all their work and talents – thank you. Finally, to the many amazing people I have had the fortune to work with over the past 18 years in both media and business, thank you for sharing your time and gifts with me.

Publisher's acknowledgements

The publisher would like to thank the following for their kind permission to reproduce their photographs:

Shutterstock.com: Pressmaster page 2, Balazs Justin page 17, IMG_191 LLC page 26, sculpies page 29, Sarah Cheriton-Jones page 32, scyther5 page 34, rangizzz pages 35 and 77, Alex Kalmbach page 37, Dmitry Bruskov page 49, Maria Skaldina page 50, Laurin Rinder page 58, T-Design page 60, Lisa F. Young page 78, Ljupco Smokovski page 82, Maxim Blinkov page 83, Sirikorn Techatraibhop page 85, Robert Kneschke page 89, John McCormick page 94, Monkey Business Images page 95, Michael Felix Photography page 99, Karramba Production page 100, Maridav page 102, Blaj Gabriel page 105, Andresr page 111.

Front cover images: Shutterstock.com: L_amica, phipatbig.

All other images © Pearson Education.

Every effort has been made to trace the copyright holders and we apologise in advance for any unintentional omissions. We would be pleased to insert the appropriate acknowledgement in any subsequent edition of this publication.

INTRODUCTION

90 per cent of the success of your presentation is determined before you stand up in front of your audience.

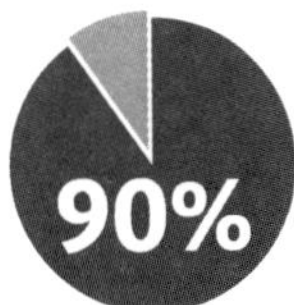

To be a successful, impactful presenter there are three steps you must take before you stand up and present to your audience.

1. You must profile your audience.
2. You must structure and shape your messages.
3. You must design visual aids.

The right approach
1. Profile your audience
2. Structure and shape your messages
3. Design visual aids

I have worked with thousands upon thousands of businesspeople from interns to CEOs, from accountants to zoologists. I have not met one single person who takes this approach.

This is the typical approach to presentations that I see:

1. **The slides are prepared first:** Steps one and two, profiling the audience and structuring and shaping the messages, are not even considered. In preparing their presentation, most presenters open their laptop and start typing data onto their slides, believing this is the only step in the process of preparing a presentation. The truth is this is fundamentally destroying your chance of being an effective presenter before you have even begun.

2. **There is no difference between the handout and the slides:** Presenters will regularly prepare a handout which they will then use as their slides and also as their notes. In reality a handout, a visual aid (slides) and your notes have three completely different purposes and all need to be prepared separately.

3. **Lack of preparation:** Because of the above approach presenters have not prepared to talk *to* their audience. They have prepared to talk *at* their audience. They have prepared to dump data. They have written that data onto their slides. Very often this is every single word they are going to speak in case they lose their way. Plus the slide is also doubling up as the handout so it needs all the information. The presenter is now:

   - speaking the written word;
   - delivering a whole heap of information with no clear messages;
   - following a structure dictated to them by their slides rather than their own natural way of thinking.

The wrong approach!

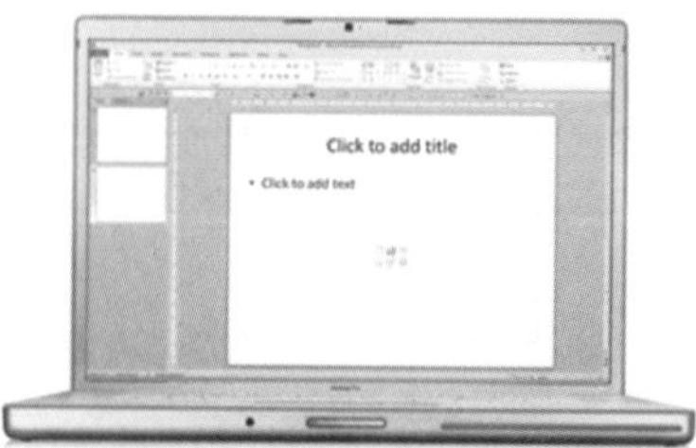

The truth about presenting

'I have to be honest with you before we go any further. Every single day I meet intelligent, educated and confident businesspeople who are letting themselves down when they stand up to make a presentation.'

Being recognised as the expert does not mean you are an expert presenter

You can be the world's leading expert in your field. You can have a BA, MA and PhD. You can be a leader in a great organisation with expertise and knowledge superior to anyone else. What all this means is you have good information, maybe even really great information. It does not mean, however, that you have the ability to present your information to an audience in an engaging and understandable way. Knowing something (having plenty of information) and delivering structured, sharp messages to an audience are two totally different skills.

Your feelings of comfort are not an indicator of how good a presenter you are

If you are at a place where presenting feels comfortable for you, I think that is great. If you believe in yourself I believe there is nothing greater. However, the truth is that feelings of confidence and comfort are not evidence you are a good presenter. In fact they could be getting in your way and blinding you to the reality of your presentation skills. The question is not whether you are confident and feel good. The questions you should be asking are:

1. Did I engage my audience?
2. Did I answer the one question my audience really needed?
3. Did I structure my information so it was easy to follow?
4. Did I get my point across in two words, in 200 words, or did I get it across at all?
5. Did I design my visual aids to have impact for my audience?

A great presentation is not about you, your comfort or your expertise. It's about your audience.

The first question you have to ask yourself

The first question you have to ask yourself even before you read on is – do you want to be a great presenter? Maybe you are happy being an average presenter, the same as everyone else you see. They get away with it, don't they? Surely you can too. Being a great presenter is not easy and it requires commitment and work. Do you see the value in presenting enough to put that work in?

IN THE MIND OF THE PRESENTER

I did a one-to-one presentations skills coaching session with an engineer working in a Europe-wide organisation who presents himself to hundreds of people weekly. He was telling me about his experience and his challenges when presenting. Although he was talking about nerves and a lack of experience I was not convinced this was his problem.

After I listened to him speak for a while I asked him if he saw the value in presenting. 'No,' he said. 'Presenting is pointless and a waste of my time.' I was really shocked by his reply. I genuinely couldn't believe there was a person in business today who didn't recognise how important presentations are.

So what is the value in presenting skilfully?

No matter what you do for a living, no matter what industry you are in and no matter what level you are at (pre-manager, manager or senior executive) you have to do some form of:

- presenting to **inform/educate;**
- presenting to **persuade/influence;**
- presenting to **ignite/motivate;**
- presenting to **sell**.

Presentation skills are critical to the success of a business. Without presentation skills, individuals are held back and businesses falter.

Every time you stand up in front of an audience, whether that is two people or 200 people, you are selling yourself, your message, your product or service. While you are doing this the audience is sitting there judging you. That judgement can be either positive or negative but there will be a judgement. You will have an impact on every audience you stand in front of. You will leave them trusting you or rejecting you based on your presentation.

A great presentation can get you promoted, win you million-pound business deals or at the very least consistently present your credibility and expertise.

A bad presentation can lose you job opportunities, handicap your ideas and tell your audience you don't know your topic or worse you don't care.

There are very real consequences to not presenting well. You will severely limit your career potential and you will lose business. That is a guarantee.

Good presentation	Bad presentation
✓ Gets you promoted	× Limits your career
✓ Wins new business	× Loses you business
✓ Communicates your credibility	× Damages your personal brand

If you are:

- **a CEO** you must inspire, motivate and lead with your words (having the job title and position is not enough to make them listen to you);
- **a sales person** you must convince someone to buy your product or service (the trick is to stop selling your product and start educating them on their problem and how your solution can help them);
- **a consultant** you must influence a room to follow your processes (you must find a way to explain these very complex approaches simply);
- **an academic** you must condense your 500-page report into clear findings (no one cares how you got there … sorry);
- **a solicitor** you have to make the law understandable (not easy when all your audience wants to know is how much will I be fined and will I go to jail if I don't pay it);
- **an accountant** you must put the 100 numbers on your spreadsheet into context (all your audience wants to know is what is the bottom line);
- **a teacher/lecturer** you must explain abstract concepts and theories to a room full of students so they can pass their exams (and that is on top of getting and keeping their attention);
- **a graduate/trainee/intern** you are at the beginning of your career, trying to prove yourself; you must showcase your ability to take something complex and make it simple (the biggest challenge is you are only getting to grips with it yourself).

In business today no matter what your job title the ability to present a message to a group of people is something everyone has to do in one form or another.

The reality is engineers don't just deal with machines and models, accountants don't just deal with numbers and solicitors don't just deal with legislation. They need to present to their co-workers and managers. They need to go out into the world and present themselves and their ideas to their clients, industry groups and regulatory agencies.

They need to know how to present with impact to do this effectively.

For a presenter to succeed he or she must figure out how to get the information out of their mind to the people in the audience in a way they will understand, remember and even act on. This is the skill of presenting. This is the skill you may not have been taught despite graduating from a top university, having a 25-year career under your belt or acquiring a very impressive job title.

Great presenters are created, not born.

The good news is you are not as bad as you think you are; you probably just need to work harder at it.

The bad news is you are not as good as you think you are; you definitely need to work harder at it.

You know who you are … at least I hope you do.

Great presenters
are created
not born

Chapter 1

Fail to prepare, prepare to fail

Microsoft estimates that there are 300 million PowerPoint users in the world, with an estimated 30 million presentations happening every day. Right now as you read this there are 1 million PowerPoint presentations being delivered somewhere in the world. I am sure there are also many thousands more using other presentation software too.

The reality is the majority of these presentations leave their audience feeling confused, frustrated or bored.

But why?

- A presentation is not a written document read out in full.
- A presentation is not you dumping what's in your head at warp speed because you can't find your point (probably because you haven't prepared one) at a poor audience that can't escape.
- A presentation is not you presenting to prove how great you are or to show your boss how much you know.

This is not presenting yet this is what most people do. It is for this reason presentations fail, some spectacularly and with irreversible consequences.

A great presentation is about:

- figuring out what questions your audience need an answer to;
- deciphering and selecting the key messages from all your data that will answer the audience's questions fittingly;
- ensuring for the limited time you get your chance to speak you are getting those messages across, clearly, understandably and in a way that will get results.

In order to present with impact you must treat the presentation step as one totally unique from writing a written document or putting together a handout. A presentation is in need of a process of its own.

In order to prepare and deliver an impactful presentation you must **step away from the computer!**

Before you go near your computer and more specifically your slideware you must:

1. Profile your audience
2. Structure and shape your messages
3. Design visual aids

The right approach

1. Profile your audience
2. Structure and shape your messages
3. Design visual aids

It is this simple three-step approach you are going to take away and be able to implement immediately after reading this book.

Before I detail this approach there is one serious issue we have to address right now and that is a lack of preparation. No matter what the approach a lack of preparation is the biggest obstacle to presentation success.

I will give you the three-step approach and I guarantee it will transform your presentations but only if you do the preparation work required. The approach I am going to give you is:

- not a quick fix to a lack of proper content crafting;
- not a miracle cure for a lack of rehearsal;
- not a substitute for the work you must do to be a great presenter.

> **'Only one who devotes himself to a cause with his whole strength and soul can be a true master. For this reason mastery demands all of a person.'**
>
> ALBERT EINSTEIN

Fail to prepare, prepare to fail

There is a very common statement people make to me regularly on my courses:

> *'It's weird, when I am prepared properly for my presentations, they go okay. I mean I am still a bit nervous but they go quite well and at the end I feel good and I get good feedback. But when I am not prepared properly it is a disaster! I go blank, I lose my way, and I am sooo nervous. What do you think it is? Maybe I don't have enough charisma ... can you give me that?'*

My thoughts on hearing this ... seriously ... charisma ... you think that's your problem? That my friend is the least of your problems!

Why don't presenters prepare properly for presentations?

I have asked myself and many of my participants this question over the years to try to get to the bottom of it.

What I have discovered is there are three main reasons why presenters defend their lack of preparation:

1. The urban myth.

2. I do prepare – in my head.

3. I don't have enough time.

They go a little something like this:

THE URBAN MYTH

> *'Our CEO here doesn't ever prepare for presentations. He just gets up and speaks off the cuff. If he can do it, why can't I?!'*

This is a regular preparation justification I hear. There is always a person identified who they believe doesn't prepare and therefore conclude that preparation is not necessary. They also back this up with the argument that they themselves are in a senior position therefore it seems unnecessary for them to have to prepare at their level. Sound fair?

In most of the companies in which I have worked the person referred to as presenting off the cuff has spent between two and four hours with me preparing for the referenced presentation. They just didn't tell anyone about it. You cannot present well without preparing. That is a fact.

I DO PREPARE – IN MY HEAD

I love this one. Many people tell me how they spent time thinking about and planning their presentation and I get very excited before they explain all this preparation took place in their head. This is probably the worst place in the world to prepare.

In your head it will all go swimmingly. You will never um and ah in your own head. You will never go blank in your own head. You will never get nervous in your own head. You will be brilliant in your own head.

Preparing a presentation in your head is like trying to learn to drive a car on a bicycle – completely crazy and ultimately futile.

I DON'T HAVE ENOUGH TIME

I have only one thing to say about this: you do have enough time if you think it's important enough.

Let me address this right now. The biggest myth on this planet is that you can present well and feel confident with little or no preparation. Honestly, what are you expecting to happen if you:

- throw the slides together the night before and read them on the bus or train that morning;
- poach another person's presentation;
- take three presentations already on the system, extract a few slides from each, leaving you with a presentation that actually belongs to three other people?

If you do what I have just described this is what you look like from the audience's point of view:

- You let the slides lead the talk.
- You spend all your time talking to the slides and not the audience.
- You speak in a monotone voice with no breaks and no rhythm because you are *reading not speaking*.
- You make no eye contact with the audience. Your focus is on the slides and surviving in one piece.
- You have body language that says 'I don't want to be here'. You fidget with a pointer or clicker while fumbling through slides and notes.
- You fill the slides with too many bullet points and full sentences.
- You do not have a logical flow or structure. You try to communicate too much, too fast, causing information overload.
- You do not have clear, structured messages.

Off the cuff

When I was in school there was a girl in my class who told me she never studied for exams. Despite this assertion she used to get straight As. This baffled me because when I didn't study I got Ds. I never questioned at the time she might be lying to me; in fact, I concluded she was smarter than me.

It took me a long time to realise my mistake. There is no such thing as a student who gets straight As and doesn't study. Similarly, there is no such thing as a presenter who talks naturally (looks like they are talking off the cuff) and is successful at delivering their message without proper preparation. *It is not possible.* It may look off the cuff or natural but that is because the presenter has spent time preparing it to look that way.

A presenter must prepare and prepare effectively for the end result to be a success. I didn't know this truth in school when I thought (or wished) you could get straight As without effort. I meet people every day who don't understand this reality applies to presenting.

There is nothing live about live television

Early in my career I worked as a presenter on the BBC show *Live and Kicking*. It was a live three-hour show that ran every Saturday for nine months from September to May. We presented on air for approximately two hours, allowing for cartoons and other programmes we showed as part of the three-hour show.

We prepared in exactly the same way for the entire nine-month run. It went something like this.

THURSDAY

The *Live and Kicking* week began on a Thursday at midday. I, my co-host Steve, the producers and the editor would all sit in a meeting room and a detailed document called a running order of items would be handed out. This was literally how the show would run, what competitions, interviews and games we were doing and in what order. We would then go through each section in great detail and start to discuss how we would bring the text and items to life. The producers' role was to come with ideas to make each item work, but as presenters Steve and I had to figure out what we would personally and individually bring to an interview or item. This meeting ran for seven hours.

THURSDAY EVENING

On Thursday evening I would go home and start to put some structure on my items. I would work on how to introduce and end each section I was presenting. I worked on this for about two hours.

FRIDAY

Friday was a full rehearsal day from 8am to 7pm. We went into the studio where the show was transmitted from and we literally walked and talked the entire show twice. Some sections were rehearsed more than that. Every single detail from the way we walked, the way we talked and the way we interacted was rehearsed and critiqued by the production team.

FRIDAY EVENING

Friday evenings would consist of two hours of me sitting on my couch, speaking my scripts out loud, trying to link everything together and make sure it all flowed.

SATURDAY

After hair and make-up we did another full run-through of the show and even when we were on air we were continually rehearsing the upcoming items before we got to them.

After the show or the next day I would sit down and watch a recorded disc of the show in full. This was never easy to do and I rarely liked what I saw but it was essential to see myself as I was, rather than how I felt I was.

What always amazed me was how *unreliable* my feelings were. I had many Saturdays where I felt I was lacking in confidence and was very surprised watching myself back to see this was not visible to the audience. Equally I had Saturdays where I felt very self-assured and again when I watched it back in fact I was lacking a spark on those days.

MONDAY

Our post-show meeting would begin at 2pm with the ratings for that week. We would get a breakdown of the three-hour show in 15-minute segments and we would know exactly who watched which part. We would then go back over each section in detail to see why things did or didn't work.

There is no easing off!

Each week, without exception, for nine months this was my routine for preparing for *Live and Kicking*. The reason I am telling you this is because I would like you to understand the consistent approach to preparation we took on a weekly basis. At no time was it felt we could ease off because we knew our stuff and had been doing the show for a while.

Thursday meeting	7
Thursday evening	2
Friday rehearsal	11
Friday evening	2
Saturday morning	3
Saturday show	1
Monday debrief	4

Preparation

The best and most powerful presenters make the time to prepare.

To create a clear and influential presentation and to give you the confidence you need as a speaker you must schedule the time to research, develop, organise, flesh out, script and rehearse your presentation.

Please note the recommended time to prepare a brand new presentation from scratch is a minimum of ***10 hours for every 1 hour presenting****.*

This is an example of how I prepared for a talk I gave to a brand new client. It was a 60-minute talk. It was not a completely new presentation as 60 per cent of the content was already prepared from a previous talk.

PRACTICE WHAT YOU PREACH

Monday – I completely ignore all my own advice and approach because I feel I am pretty sure of my audience and their needs. I grab a few of my old presentations and start cutting and pasting slides into what I feel will work. I print these off and plan to talk through them on Tuesday.

Tuesday – I spend my lunch time between clients speaking my slides out loud. It is not working, it is not flowing, I am getting confused and a little overwhelmed at this point. I can only spend one hour on it, then I have to leave it.

Thursday – I realise I have to go back to the beginning and follow the approach so I send an email to Suzanne, who is my contact for the talk, and I ask her the audience profile questions (I will explain these in detail later). Suzanne responds very quickly, which is great, and now I am clear on my audience and what they need. I establish my goal and then it all becomes clear. I plan a new structure for my content.

Sunday – As I am now two days behind on where I should be I have to work Sunday on my slides. I need to get 14 new slides designed for the talk and they need to be sent to Ed, my slide design guy, so they will be ready in time for rehearsal.

Wednesday – I rehearse my talk in full after a day's training.

Friday – I rehearse my talk in full in my office.

Monday – I rehearse my talk in full after a day's training.

Wednesday – Talk day – I do one rehearsal on the morning of the presentation.

There is no shortcut to presentation success

I know some of you reading this book work 12-hour days just to meet the demands of your day-to-day job. I know you have partners and children with whom you like to spend time in the evenings and at weekends. I know you want to prepare but the problem is time. Finding the time to prepare for a presentation is an enormous challenge for many professionals.

I can't solve your workload problems but I can tell you if you are ploughing through presentations that aren't working for you then you need to prepare properly. Preparing for your presentations must become a vital item on your to do list, not the thing you put on the long finger or leave to the last minute because you have too much else to do.

People tell me all the time that when they prepare properly they perform very well. A lot of the obstacles that arise with presenting become inconsequential with preparation.

Fundamental preparation steps like rehearsing your talk out loud a minimum of three times before you do it for real is vital for presentation success. If you don't rehearse your presentation in full out loud it will be full of hesitation, *ums*, *ah*s and long drawn-out sentences. You will look unsure of your messages and as if you don't know what you're talking about.

I have devoted an entire chapter to presentation preparation in the hope of convincing you how worthwhile and essential preparation is. You can be a really great presenter, but you have to prepare.

Chapter 2

It's not about self-survival

What is a great presentation?

Let's start at the very beginning. What is a great presentation?

You know it when you see it, don't you, but it can be very hard to pinpoint what you're seeing. Usually we attribute a great presentation to the presenter's personality, charisma or style. It seems that great presenters have some intangible quality that is just out of reach.

This is simply not true and once you examine what a great presenter is actually doing you realise it has very little to do with the individual presenting.

Let me tell you exactly what a great presenter does:

1. A great presenter begins the presentation with the first question the audience wants answered. They start with the audience's needs, thoughts and feelings. This is what is called the point of engagement.
2. A great presenter then takes their audience by the hand (metaphorically of course) through their data by the most direct, easy, jargon-free, enjoyable and understandable route possible.
3. The end point of the presentation is the result. This means the audience are thinking and doing what the presenter planned for.

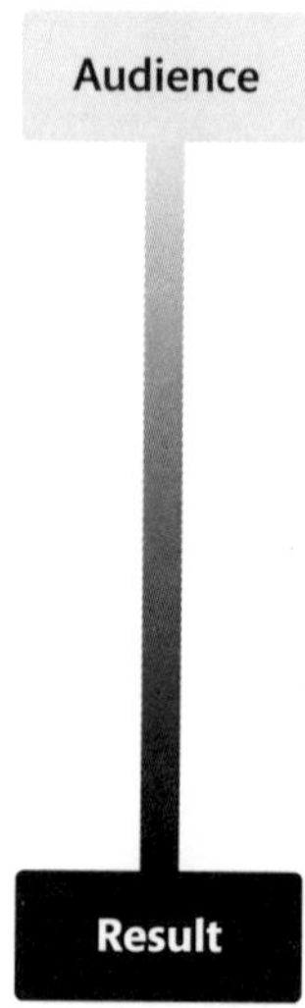

This is the point where:

- the audience understands the concept;
- the audience has bought into the idea;
- the audience recognises the messages of the presentation and how these messages relate to them.

A great presentation grabs the mind of the audience at the beginning, navigates them through all the various parts, themes and ideas easily, never letting go, and then gets them to the point of action or result.

Very few people do this. Most people take a path similar to that shown below.

Most presenters don't consider the audience and their needs properly (doing so in your head doesn't count) and start a presentation from their own point of view, their starting place. They start the presentation at the point they think is important and then they simply dump data in all directions. In other words they talk about their topic. Sure, isn't that what you're supposed to do?

While they talk about their topic, among their data are their messages and some very important points. Unfortunately these messages get lost in a fog of facts.

The audience has to work very hard to unearth the point of the talk and understand the data being flung at them. In most cases an audience is not prepared to work this hard. In some presentation scenarios an audience may not even know why they should listen in the first place.

The sum of the parts

The skill of presenting involves two distinct, individual parts you must consider separately: communication and delivery.

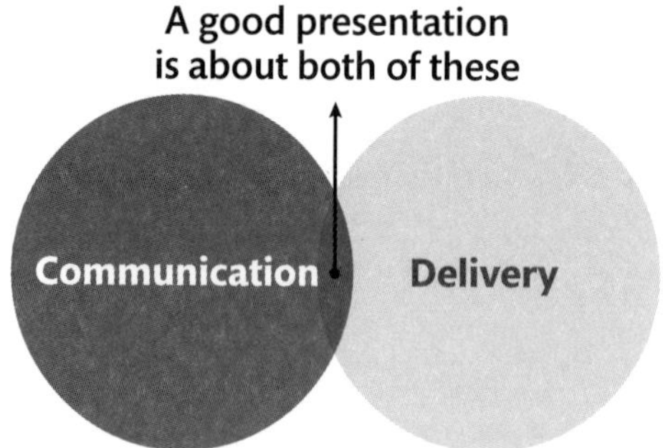
A good presentation
is about both of these
Communication
Delivery

This is a slide I use in my talks to convey the message that in order for a presentation to be great it must give equal weighting to both communication and delivery.

Most people when they think of a presentation tend to focus on the second circle – delivery skills. This is the part of the presentation where you have to stand in front of the audience. This is the scary part. This is the part where you don't want to embarrass yourself.

There are hundreds of presentation skills courses out there offering absurd tips and tricks (no offence) to survive this part of a presentation. My personal favourites include but are not limited to:

1. Stare at the back of the room. (You will look crazy.)
2. Imagine everyone naked. (This is definitely a really fun game but I would save it for the Christmas party.)
3. Hold a pen. (You will fidget with it, drop it or click it.)

A presentation is not about self-survival . . . or is it?

Self-survival

Actually, a presentation *is* about self-survival and this is what you have to change if you are going to have any chance of having a positive impact on an audience.

We are all afraid

Every single human being on this planet who presents is afraid of the same thing, *not being enough*. Not being smart enough, confident enough or knowledgeable enough.

They are afraid of being found out. They are afraid they won't look like they have done their research or job properly. They are afraid of being asked a question they don't know the answer to.

This means they approach their presentation in self-survival mode. The problem with this mode is it is about you the presenter, surviving the experience of presenting rather than putting the audience first and creating a positive and engaging experience for them.

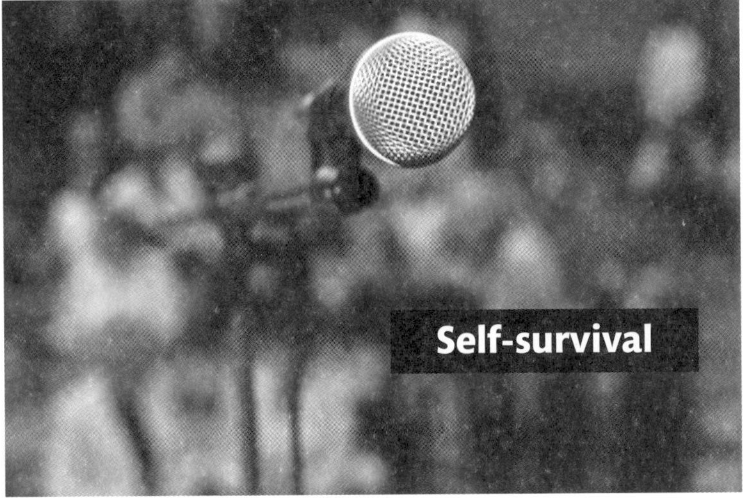

Presenting is scary, but in order to deliver a successful presentation you will have to get out of the self-survival mindset.

Ownership

The only way to be successful in a presentation is to take ownership of the experience you are creating for your audience.

Firstly you have to make a decision to take the focus off you and make your audience number one. You must make them the most important person in the room.

Secondly you must get to grips with your words and your message. Owning what you say is vital to being credible and authentic. If you don't own what you are saying all you are doing is impersonally reading data.

Ownership

It quite simply comes down to ownership of the experience you are creating for the audience.

The best approach

The *self-survival* approach – the audience is doing the work for the presenter

If the presenter approaches the presentation preparation from a place of self-survival this is typically what they will do:

- The presenter will gather all their data together.
- The presenter will then deliver the raw data directly to the audience and feel relieved their work is done.
- The audience must now take the data, analyse it and figure out how it relates to them.

With this approach both the presenter and the audience is left feeling a little relieved that it's all over, but ultimately dissatisfied and frustrated.

The *ownership approach* – the presenter is doing the work for the audience

- The presenter will gather all their data together.
- The presenter will then think about the specific audience they are going to talk to and what they need. They will analyse their own data and prepare tailored messages that are easy to understand.
- The presenter will then deliver powerful and impactful messages which the audience can easily digest and comprehend.

With this approach the audience feels like the presenter has climbed inside their head and is giving them what they really need from the talk.

Win-win

Presentations are a vital component in building a business relationship with a client.

When you present there is the potential for one of three outcomes:

1. Win-Lose
2. Lose-Win
3. Win-Win

You can leave your presentation feeling like a winner but your audience may have lost out. They were not engaged or talked to. They were simply subjected to an hour of data overload and irrelevance. This is a win-lose situation.

There is a scenario where the audience feels they got what they wanted and needed but the presenter feels a loss of integrity because they didn't present themselves the way they had hoped. For example, the audience may only care about cost but the presenter knows quality is a big issue but fails to get this point across and fears long-term consequences. This is a lose-win situation.

In presentations, as in life, both of these scenarios will breed long-term resentment and frustration for both the presenter and audience. This is not good business because this is not good relationship building.

The ending you want from any presentation is a win-win situation. Both the presenter and the audience must feel they have won while also meeting the needs of each party.

Can you convert the Unconvertible?

Can you always achieve a win-win outcome with every audience? No, you can't. You can only create a win-win with an audience who has something to gain or lose from your presentation. Let me explain.

The members of any audience you find yourself in front of will always fall into one of three categories:

- The Converted
- The Unconvertible
- The Floater

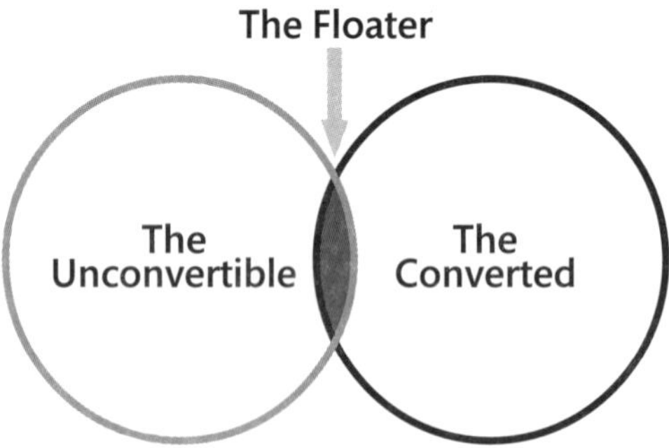

The Converted

Someone you have already influenced successfully and is doing, thinking or feeling the things you want. You have already achieved a win-win outcome. These people may be in the room but they are not your audience for this presentation.

The Unconvertible

When your audience is in this position they cannot be influenced no matter what you do. This could be due to a number of factors including:

1. They are simply not interested because what you are saying is not relevant to them.
2. They may have had a bad experience with you/your company and have no wish to engage with you again.
3. There may be a better offer from some another company/person.

The only time you can engage this group is if they move into the Floater position.

The Floaters

The group open to being influenced by your presentation. Your aim is to turn them into the Converted. The Floaters are open to listening to you. The reason they are not converted already is because they have a question, maybe many questions, that you have not addressed. The only way to move them from Floater to Converted is to identify the questions they need an answer to (the right questions) and address them to their satisfaction. This is not as easy as it sounds and many times the presenter will identify the wrong questions and fail in the presentation.

Converting the Floaters

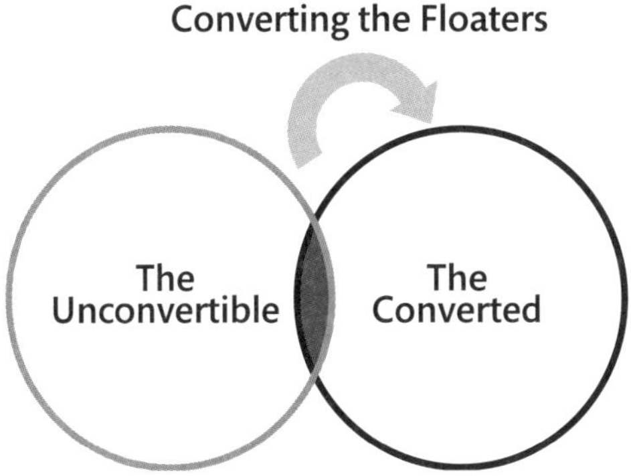

IN THE MIND OF THE PRESENTER

A company, let's call them Company X, called me to work with them recently as they had lost a very big pitch to provide a health care scheme for staff in a large multinational company. We examined what happened. Company X assumed the potential client was concerned with price so they focused on this hoping it would influence the client, who was in the Floater position. Company X did make the best offer in terms of price so they were very taken aback when they did not win the business.

After contacting the potential client for feedback it turned out cost was not the most important question this multinational had. Its main concern was how staff would cope with a new company taking over with a new scheme. Company X did not address this in any detail. It was covered in one bullet point on a slide in the middle of the presentation.

Company X failed to win the business (turn the Floater into the Converted) because they didn't answer the most important question for the potential client.

Their presentation failed because Company X was talking about the wrong thing. They were answering the wrong questions.

In order to turn the Floater into the Converted you must know why the Floater is still floating and make them understand why they should convert. This is the art of a great presentation.

This is where I come in

I know you probably have some idea of what makes a good presentation (you have sat through enough bad ones). However, I also believe you probably don't completely know how to create a great presentation. For example, how do you turn your data into a series of engaging, impactful messages? How do you turn the Floater into the Converted?

This is where I come in. I will give you the tools and show you how to create a great presentation. I will give you a simple three-step approach that will structure and shape any data you have into an engaging and influential presentation.

But first we must start with the basics.

If great presentations are made up of two parts - communication and delivery - then we must look at both of these in detail. Let's start with communication.

Chapter 3

The missing ingredient

What is communication?

We all have different ideas about what communication is defined as, but it's really quite straightforward.

Communication is simply **creating understanding from your raw information.**

Good communication

When someone is communicating very well they do three things:

1. They tell their audience why they should listen.
2. They put their data together in a meaningful way like a great story. They also use examples and simple language to make sure the audience can understand the concepts.
3. Finally, the presenter ensures the messages are memorable by the correct use of visuals and stories.

They are doing three very simple things:

1. Hooking
2. Telling a story
3. Being remembered

Good communication

1. Hooking
2. Telling a story
3. Being remembered

A slide I use in my talks to illustrate the three simple things that great communicators do.

Communication at school

We all experienced our best examples of great communicators in our classrooms at school. Think back to the one great teacher you had among the many average educators. What made that teacher so great? The reason they stood out is because they were not just dumping data and theory on you, they were communicating.

If you look even closer you will see what all memorable educators have in common:

- They made it about you.
- They made the data easy and digestible.
- They had clear messages and points.
- They structured their data.
- They really believed in their message.
- They controlled their nerves.
- They were prepared.
- They were open to you and they talked to you directly.
- They did not use the slides as their notes or crutch.
- They looked at you.

They made it easy, and they made it about you.

A great presentation	
✓ Making the information relevant/examples	✓ In control of nerves
✓ Easy to understand	✓ Good flow
✓ Clear points	✓ Open in body language
✓ Structured	✓ No text-heavy slides
✓ Interest/passion	✓ Eye contact

Great presentations tend to follow the checklist above.

Great presenting is simply great communication

Great communication is about making sure your audience engages, understands and remembers your key points. It is about taking the driest of topics and making it relevant, interesting and even enjoyable for your audience. Great communication is about you doing all the work to create a great experience for your audience.

To be a great communicator you must know your audience inside and out. You must talk to your audience about them and things that interest them. To explain your ideas you must find great stories, examples and analogies your audience can relate to. You must talk with passion and interest in your own subject.

Great communication takes work on the part of the presenter as you must research, develop, organise, structure, shape and rehearse your presentation. Communication is the missing ingredient in all the business presentations I see today. Presenters are standing up and simply transmitting data rather than taking the time to tailor that data to the needs of their audience.

The real X factor

This is what I was told by a business development manager about his team recently:

'The problem with my team is they have no impact. I need them to have the X factor.'

When I then had the team in a room together I asked them why they felt they needed training. They repeated back to me what their superior had told me. *'I have no impact; I don't have the X factor.'*

I asked the team to tell me exactly what their messages were. Not one of them was clear in their answer. I asked their manager what value they were offering to a potential client. He looked at me blankly. *'It's hard to put into words,'* he said.

The X factor was not what was missing here. The team I was training did have value to offer but they hadn't developed a message to sell it. There was no clarity in their presentations.

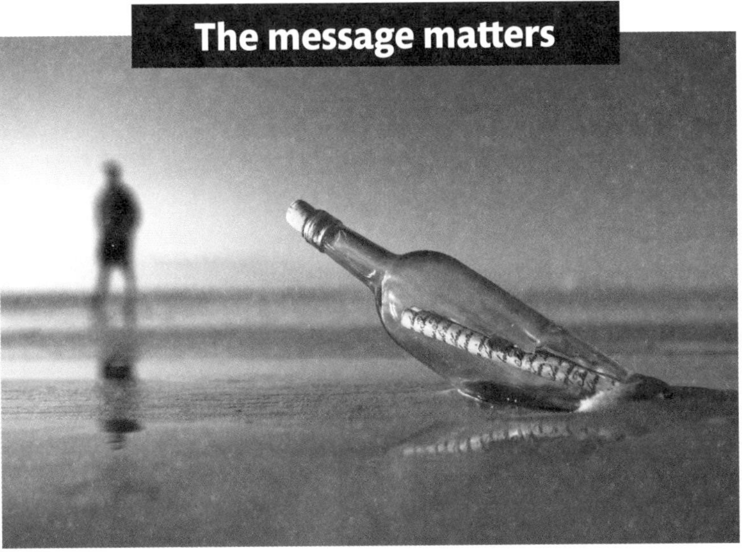

How can a team feel empowered and passionate about a product or service that is not completely clear to them?

The reality is this team were paralysed. In trying to motivate and develop his staff the manager had actually created a situation where the team felt powerless. Despite their college educations and business experience their presentation skills were insufficient.

If you are a business development manager reading this I want you to ask yourself these questions:

- Could you tell me in a couple of sentences why I should buy from you?
- If I asked your team what they were offering of value would they *all* give me the same answer?
- Do your team believe in your product or service?

Your potential clients cannot be reached by staff who feel incompetent or worse powerless to fix the problem of not having the elusive X factor.

Companies believe this intangible quality, the X factor, is the secret to presentation success. The truth is the X factor can be a matter of taste, moral background, viewpoints and preferences. The secret to presentation success is much more real; it is good communication delivered by a confident individual who believes in himself and his offering. This is the X factor you should be focusing on.

Chapter 4

Hook your audience

What's in it for me?

The first step to being a great presenter is to stand in the shoes of your audience and figure out what they need.

Before a presentation, any audience anywhere in the world is always thinking two things:

1. How long do I have to sit here for?

2. And ... what's in it for me?

What your audience really want to know is: Why should I listen to this presentation?

At the end of the day people have their own self-interests at heart. They want to know what is in it for them!

You need to answer this question. You need to tell your audience why they should listen to you. You need to tell your audience the value of your information to them.

This is what is called a hook.

You cannot assume your audience will listen. You cannot assume they want to listen. Maybe they do, maybe they don't. Maybe they will, maybe they won't. There are a lot of maybes.

I have come across presenters who tell me there is no reason for their audience to listen to them as their presentation has no real value.

If you don't have anything of value to say to your audience please stop talking and sit down.

It's not about you

You need to stop talking *at* your audience about *you*, *your* company or *your* topic.

You need to start talking *to* them about *them*, *their reality* and how your company or concept will be of value.

The secret to great presenting is to talk to your audience about them rather than at them about you.

Why should they listen?

Are you funny? If you are, please do tell a joke. Are you charismatic? If you are, go forth and charm.

The good news is neither of the above has anything to do with whether an audience will hang on your every word or not.

Your audience will engage with you and listen to you only if there is a reason for them to listen, for example:

1. If they are **sincerely interested** in what you have to say.
2. If they know there is a **benefit** to what you have to say.
3. If they feel there will be a **negative consequence** to not listening to what you have to say.

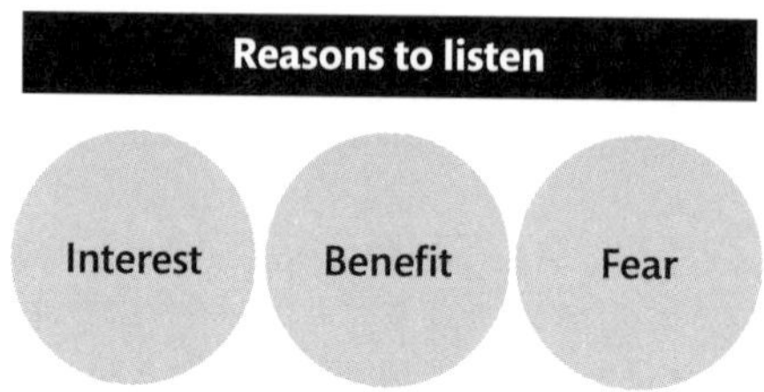

What reason are you giving your audience to listen to your message?

The remote control test

I would like you to think for a second about the way you watch television. You are sitting on your couch channel surfing. You change to a new channel, you ask yourself: Is this interesting (interest), worth watching (benefit)? Do I need to watch this (fear)? Eh no. Next!

OK, now imagine every single member of your audience has a remote control in their hand. Now imagine they have ten other channels to switch to and if you lose them you will not get them back. How long do you think you have with your presentation in its current format before you lose them to another channel?

Introductions are important

Audiences make the decision to listen to you *very quickly*. Your audience will decide if your presentation is interesting, of benefit or if there is the fear factor in the first …

Stop talking about what you're going to talk about and just talk about it.

A lot of presenters spend their introductions and the majority of their presentation telling their audience:

- what they are going to tell them;
- what they already know;
- what they don't want to know.

This has got to stop right now.

You have to cut to the chase, get to the point and be direct. You need to inspire your audience, engage them, and let them know this presentation is worth listening to and fast. When it is your turn to talk please say something interesting straight away.

The key to a presentation is getting the beginning just right.

Getting the beginning just right

This is the way an engineer started his presentation to the board of management about the need to standardise the company's processes:

> **'As I was doing some research for this presentation, I read the city of Baltimore burnt to the ground in 1904. The tragedy is it didn't have to.**
>
> **Firefighters from nearby DC, New York, and Virginia all responded, but weren't able to help because their hose couplings wouldn't fit on the Baltimore hydrants - no standard had yet been set. The firefighters helplessly watched as the city burned.**
>
> **Like Baltimore, our organisation will suffer if we don't standardise our processes.'**

This is the opening of a speech to a group of parents to raise awareness in a community about school security:

> **'Tobacco, alcohol, a knife . . .**
>
> **These items were seized in a random search of final year students' lockers in our school last week.'**

What about an agenda?

Imagine you turned on the radio in your car to your favourite station and the DJ was telling you what was coming up in the next hour. They began:

2.01pm we have the news

2.06pm we have an ad break

2.09pm we have the sports news

2.11pm there is going to be some banter between the DJ and a caller

2.12pm we will play a pop song

2.15pm we will play a love song

2.16pm we will take another ad break …

Have you switched over to another station yet?

They would **never** do this because they wouldn't have any listeners.

A formal agenda would make for a very strange radio show indeed, and in a presentation setting it can turn your audience off almost immediately.

A radio station will pick the best bits coming up in the next hour and try and hook you in and keep you listening for as long as possible.

For example:

'Coming up in the next hour, we will be playing our mystery voice and if you guess right this hour you win €5,000. We are going to play last night's number one and of course, we are going to give you all the latest celebrity gossip.'

A lot of presenters begin their presentation with an agenda. *'Thank you for the opportunity to talk to you today, and before I start, I would like to thank all of the following ... (insert list). In my talk today, I would like to address the following topics ... (insert list) and, of course, all of this will be written word for word on the slides.'*

The problem with agendas is they are long and boring to get through for the presenter and can give the audience an option to decide not to listen at certain points, if at all. If you want people to know what's coming up give them the highlights to keep them interested or tell them what value they will walk away with. They don't need a list of everything you are going to talk about.

You don't get a second chance to make a first impression

I cannot stress how important the beginning of your presentation is. The stronger the hook the more durable the audience's engagement will be. It is not easy to get someone to listen to you, but if you make sure they really understand the value of your information and what it can do for them you will succeed in getting their attention.

You do not need to employ any out-of-the-ordinary antics like juggling or joke-telling at the beginning of your presentation to get attention. I have seen so many of these tricks go horribly wrong and the presenter doesn't recover from the bad start.

All you have to do is answer one very simple question for your audience:

'Why should I listen to your presentation?'

Chapter 5

What goes where?

Presentation structures

The presentation structures I typically see fall into three categories:

The Mystery Tour

The idea with a mystery tour is that the guide knows exactly where they are going but the audience hasn't got a clue. This may be fun if you are on a team bonding day but in a presentation audiences do not favour this approach. They are not willing to wait till the end for the best bit, to get what they need or understand why they should listen.

The Maze

In this case the audience has no idea where the presentation is going and the presenter seems very confused as well. The presenter thought they had a clear path worked out in their head (remember that one) before they stood up, alas now the clear path is more of a labyrinth: 'No, wait hang on. No, not that way, sorry, I seem to have lost my way. Hang on … Let's try this way … Eh no. Any questions?'

Back to the Future

I recently attended a presentation about the budget for this year. The presenter spent three-quarters of the presentation talking about the budget for 2007. I was very confused. I asked her afterwards why she took this approach. She told me she wanted to put things into context. Giving a detailed background to support an eventual conclusion is not what your audience wants. They are sitting there thinking, 'What's the point of this?' They want the result, the solution, the answer to their question and they want it now. Once you give them this you can then go back to the background, contextualise or give your perspective.

The wrong way around

Most people when they structure presentations do so using what is called deductive reasoning.

Deductive reasoning moves from a general premise to a more specific conclusion. This type of presentation structure:

1. begins with a general overview, background/intro to the presenter and company;
2. goes into detail about the topics, covering all possible areas;
3. finally, right at the end, usually gives an executive summary slide that answers the question the audience had.

This is a very legitimate approach but you really must ask yourself if your audience is going to wait until the end to get what they need. Would you wait that long? This approach may be fine for a book or a written document because people are choosing to read it at their leisure or dip in and out at certain points, but for a presentation this is a very uncertain approach.

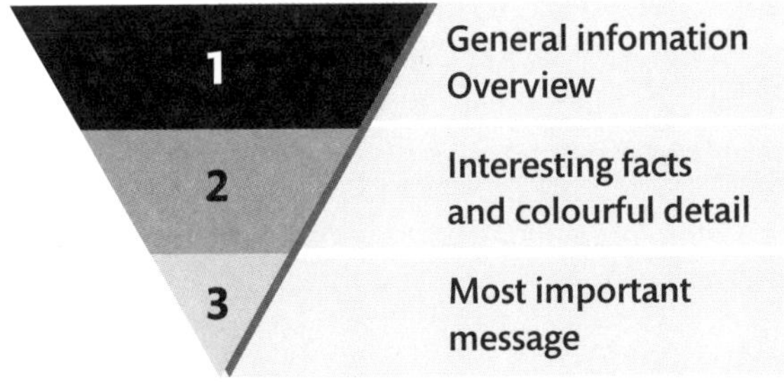

While the structure outlined above might seem like a logical way to lay out your information in a presentation, it is actually the completely wrong way to approach it!

Now here is the good news, you can transform this presentation structure in two easy steps.

Turn it right side up

You have to start your talk with your conclusion or your executive summary.

1. You must start with your most relevant and engaging point for the audience. This is what is called *inductive* reasoning. Inductive reasoning moves from the specific to the more general yet relevant material.

2. Once you have hooked the audience in the first 45 seconds by giving them what they need, you have to keep them. As you go through the facts, data and more general information you must link it back and make sure the audience knows why it is relevant to them. The word **you** is the most powerful word you can use in a presentation.

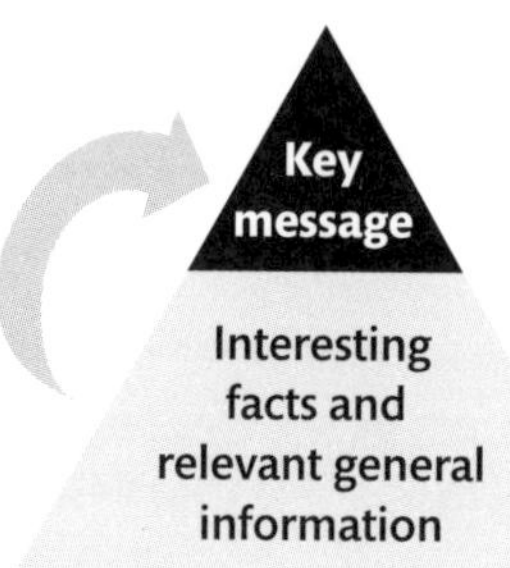

The presentation should start with the most important point and work its way down to the supporting information.

The right structure

1. It gives people a reason to listen because you are telling them the benefit or addressing the fear factor straight away.
2. It allows for repetition (you can keep linking back to the 'What's in it for me?' using the word 'you').
3. It holds people's attention. When you establish your conclusion at the beginning of your presentation, you can then weave it throughout the presentation, showing how each point that you cover relates to and supports it.

The most powerful word you can use in a presentation

Researchers at Yale have identified the 12 most powerful words in the human language proven to attract attention and stir emotion within readers. At the top of the list is the word **you**!

Using the word **you** is vital to relate your data back to the audience and what is important to them. Here are two examples of the power of the word **you**.

Before:

'We have 45 offices worldwide with 10,000 staff.' *Audience = 'So what?'*

After:

'We have 45 offices worldwide which you can access to leverage your existing business. We also have a huge support team which will be available to you with a range of languages and contacts already in place. We intend to give you a key contact in each country if you choose to do business with us.' *Audience = 'Sounds great!'*

Barack Obama, the US President, addressed supporters in Chicago after decisively winning a second term using the word 'you' to relate and engage:

> **'Tonight, more than 200 years after a former colony won the right to determine its own destiny, the task of perfecting our union moves forward.**
>
> **It moves forward because of you. It moves forward because you reaffirmed the spirit that has triumphed over war and depression, the spirit that has lifted this country from the depths of despair to the great heights of hope, the belief that while each of us will pursue our own individual dreams, we are an American family, and we rise or fall together as one nation and as one people.**
>
> **Tonight, in this election, you, the American people, reminded us that while our road has been hard, while our journey has been long, we have picked ourselves up, we have fought our way back, and we know in our hearts that for the United States of America, the best is yet to come.**
>
> **I want to thank every American who participated in this election. Whether you voted for the very first time or waited in line for a very long time, by the way we have to fix that, whether you pounded the pavement or picked up the phone, whether you held an Obama sign or a Romney sign, you made your voice heard and you made a difference.'**

What goes where?

The success of your presentation is determined by your ability to put your information together in a way that is meaningful for the audience. This is where the skill comes in.

Words and ideas have great power when they are linked together properly and in the right order.

You have to have a beginning, middle and an end not a beginning, *muddle* and an end.

The only way to avoid the muddle is to structure your data around three digestible groups of information. Any more than three and the audience will struggle to remember them.

It is vital not to overload your presentation with too many ideas and messages. Three core messages illustrated in different ways, re-visited and re-emphasised will make sure your messages are understood and remembered.

Presentation slides are not a tool for helping you structure your presentation. You must structure your data first and only after you are clear on your key messages do you then think about adding visual aids.

I am going to show you how to get your talk into this structure in the approach section of this book.

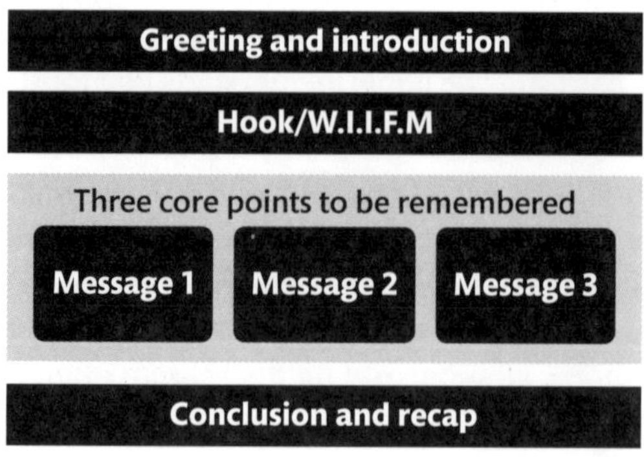

After the Introduction and Hook (What Is In It For Me?) we introduce our three core points to be remembered.

Concluding and recapping

The primacy and resonancy effect claims we remember the first thing we hear and the last thing we hear in a presentation. I have talked about how important your hook, or first 45 seconds are. This is the point where you tell your audience 'What's in it for me?' Your conclusion is also just as important as this will be the last and most recent message your audience will receive and walk away with.

Concluding a presentation is like landing a plane. There are a few ways you can do it.

1. **Crash landing**: You can crash out of the sky. You can suddenly and abruptly finish your presentation with no warning at all.
2. **Circling**: The presenter is coming to the end and realising they haven't got their message across just keeps going in the hope that they will get there at some stage. No one has ever said, I wish that presentation was longer. Only speak for your allotted time.
3. **Smooth landing**: You tell your audience what they have gained from the presentation and what action they need to take, if any. The good news is your conclusion is very similar to your hook. All you need to do is remind your audience of the key messages and why those messages are relevant to them. Thank them and ask for questions.

Chapter 6

What language should I speak?

The middle of your presentation

Let's look at the middle of your presentation.

We have looked at the beginning of a presentation and why an audience will listen. We have also looked at the conclusion. Now we need to look at the rest of a presentation.

A great presentation grabs the mind of the audience at the beginning, navigates them through all the various parts, themes and ideas, never letting go, and then gets them to the point of action or result.

Do you remember the diagram below?

The straight line in the diagram represents the part of the presentation where you must navigate your audience through your information, never letting them go, until you get them to the result you want.

The struggle is, you have to keep your audience engaged from the hook (the first 45 seconds) to the result.

The question is, how easy is your presentation to follow and do you have flow?

What kind of road are you?

I want you to imagine for a second that your presentation is like a car journey for your audience. They have to get from one destination to another and your presentation is the road they have to travel on.

- Are you a super slick motorway that allows the driver to effortlessly get from A to B without stress or hassle?
- Is your road signposted clearly to ensure your audience has a smooth journey with no wrong turns or unnecessary stops?
- Does your road make it easy and effortless to reach the place the audience wants to get to?

Or is your presentation journey more like this?

- Is your road so intertwined with so many other roads and options that the audience feels overwhelmed and confused before they even start?
- Do you have no clear signs to help the audience distinguish which road is right for them?

- Does getting to your destination leave your audience exhausted and frustrated about how long and unnecessary the journey took?

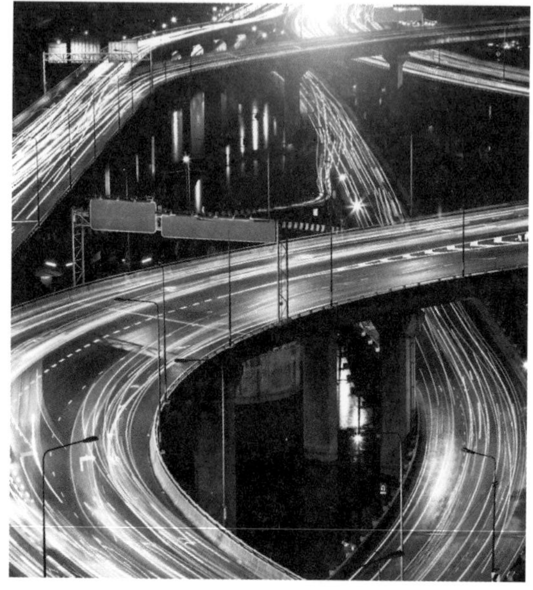

To ensure your presentation road is easy to travel down you must avoid the four presentation pitfalls.

Where it goes wrong

Here are the four main reasons your road is too difficult to travel down.

1. Not relevant

After hooking the audience in the first 45 seconds you then have to keep them.

You must be consistent with your engagement and linking throughout the talk. If at any time the audience feels your data is not relevant they will lose interest and you will lose them.

2. Data Overload

'Hello my name is ... *(insert your name here)* and I am a dataholic.'

Awareness is the first step. There is help out there; you can live a long and happy life without drowning your poor unfortunate audience in data. Sometimes it's what you don't say that matters.

3. PowerPoint

'Hello my name is ... *(ok so you know how the rest goes)*.'

I am deadly serious though, what *are* you all doing with PowerPoint?

PowerPoint is a very powerful visual aid when used *correctly*. Below is a list of what PowerPoint is NOT for.

I am going to talk to you in detail about presentation software later in the book.

DON'T USE POWERPOINT FOR:

- your notes;
- your crutch;
- a substitute for preparation;
- the handout (given before, during or after the talk);
- the PowerPoint that gets circulated to the people that weren't at the talk.

4. They don't understand

You need to speak in English and not in business-speak for your message to be understood.

I know you don't want to be seen to 'dumb things down' or speak in what you perceive to be baby talk. Dumbing down and baby talk are very different to being clear, concise and understandable. I am not asking you to dumb anything down; I am asking you to speak in a universally understood language rather than your industry dialect. In everyday conversation we speak in first-degree words. These are words that have only one meaning that everyone can understand. For example 'road' is a first-degree word. 'Infrastructure' is not.

To be understandable you have to stop:

- using concepts, acronyms and jargon without explanation;
- assuming levels of understanding that are simply not there;
- bombarding the audience with too many numbers with no context for those numbers;
- using ten sentences to say what could be said in two;
- talking about what you are going to talk about instead of just talking about it. You need to get to the point.

Facts are, of course, critical but the reality is they take time to penetrate the brain.

A mistake many professionals make is assuming their colleagues, customers or clients understand the everyday jargon they use. In most instances, this is not the case and can result in serious miscommunication and misunderstanding.

Your audience (internal and external) does not understand your industry language as much as you think or maybe in the way you think. They may have heard the acronym or come across the theory but that does not mean they understand it in the way you do.

Please don't be over-confident in your assumptions. There is a very good chance you're mistaken in assuming understanding that simply isn't there.

> **'If you can't explain it simply, you don't understand it well enough.'**
>
> ALBERT EINSTEIN, PHYSICIST

Creating understanding

The purpose of a presentation is to create understanding.

If you don't make your facts understandable you are essentially expecting your audience to:

- take on board a catalogue of data;
- assimilate the data immediately with no real context;
- reach the same conclusion you have reached.

(And all of this in 20 minutes.)

The onus is **never** on the audience, it is on the speaker to keep the listener engaged and keep things clear.

You must know your audience and how they will interpret what you are saying. Something that is incredibly natural and everyday to you may not be to them. You must speak to your audience in a language they can understand.

You have to step back from your own assumptions. If in doubt start at the beginning and make sure everyone understands.

To ensure engagement throughout and to make sure you are creating understanding you must avoid the four presentation pitfalls (above) and always do the following:

- Use first-degree words (everyday language) to explain your messages and concepts before you start using technical terms or industry jargon.
- Relate your information to how it affects your audience.
- Use real-life examples, stories or analogies to explain your concepts and bring your facts to life.

In case you don't know, first-degree words are words with only one meaning.

The power of a picture

A concept is an abstract general idea that could have many meanings. 'Sustainability' is a concept. I don't think anyone actually knows what that word means. Children and adults think in pictures and concrete thoughts rather than general ideas.

We go through years of education and all we are taught is how to memorise data and concepts. Only a very small percentage of teachers take those concepts and make them stick, make us understand and remember them.

Great presenting is about the creation of understanding. Presenting concepts to an audience and assuming they will be able to take the general abstract ideas and understand them as you do is senseless and ultimately ineffective.

You, the presenter, must take the concepts and make them real. You must present them so the audience can touch them, taste them and feel them.

People relate easily (and emotionally) to stories, examples, analogies and case studies. More importantly, people remember them. Our brains are hardwired for story. Story was how cultures were passed from generation to generation. Stories are interesting, easy to listen to and you remember the message. If you have an important message, concept or idea that must be remembered by your audience concentrate on telling a story or finding one concrete example to support your point. Facts are important and can even be critical but they penetrate the brain very slowly - remember learning your times tables or your French verbs.

Stories make facts speak. They give them an emotional context. They make facts digestible and appetising. As well as the facts entering the brain more quickly, in the process you become more human, more approachable and more audience-friendly. The best speakers reach into their bag of stories and examples and this is what brings their presentations to life. This is what connects them to the audience.

Chapter 7

The three steps

Over the next few pages I want to show you *The Presentation Book* approach. This is a time-efficient and structured way to prepare for your presentations in three easy steps. This approach is tried and tested and if followed it guarantees results.

Changing your golf grip

If you are a golfer and wish to improve your game you might go to a professional to ask for advice. That professional may tell you to move your hand to slightly change your grip, which will in turn improve your swing. This new grip is going to feel very uncomfortable for the first few weeks because you are used to the old grip.

Up to now you have been preparing and delivering your presentations in a certain way and I am going to come along and change your approach just a little. It is going to feel weird at first and may even go against what you thought.

Please remember my aim is to make you a better presenter and a slight change in your approach to presenting could make all the difference.

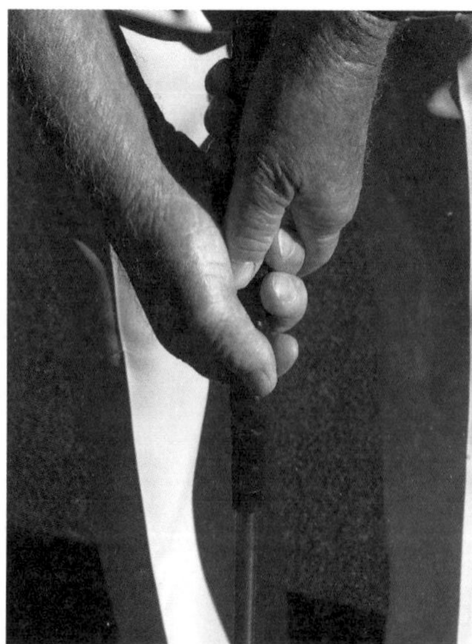

Although it might feel uncomfortable at first, it will all be worthwhile going forward.

One step at a time

The Presentation Book approach is like building a house. You have to follow a series of logical steps to move from one stage to another.

To build a house you must:

1. design it;
2. construct it;
3. fit it out.

You cannot move to step 2 until you have completed step 1; you cannot move to step 3, until you have completed step 2.

The Presentation Book approach is similar in that it involves three logical steps:

1. **Profile your audience:** This is where you understand your audience and what they need.
2. **Structure and shape your messages**: This is where you research your data and edit it into three clear messages for your audience.
3. **Design visual aids:** Now that you know what your messages are you find a way to make them as visual and understandable as possible.

The right approach
1. Profile your audience
2. Structure and shape your messages
3. Design visual aids

What I would like to do now is take you through the approach.

The most important thing to remember as you read through the approach is that these three steps need to happen **before** you go near your computer or slideware.

APPROACH STEP 1
Profile your audience

AUDIENCE PROFILING – ORLA

My name is Orla and I am 37 years old, a socially active, fun-loving, sexy female.

I love to shop for clothes. For the family I look to Next and I occasionally indulge myself at an upmarket department store for that something special.

My family are fussy about food and we generally love M&S and also try to find better value at Tesco.

I feel my home tastes are modern and contemporary, and my husband and I are hoping to move to a more exclusive area when property prices allow it.

A good night for us consists of a reliable babysitter, hard to find, and a meal for two at Pizza Express and occasionally a movie.

My children, Fergus (8) and Anna (6), recently saw Finding Nemo *and we love building our home DVD library. My children are my life.*

'Orla' was my audience and I had to make sure that everything I talked about was relevant to her.

I went to work for a radio station and I was given this piece of paper on my first day. I was told that no matter what I was talking about I had to make sure I was talking about it in relation to Orla (above).

I was always aware that every television or radio show I worked on had a specific audience, but I had never seen it written down so clearly. This is what is called *profiling the audience.*

Audience profiling is the act of really knowing who you're talking to. Audience profiling is understanding the needs of your audience beforehand, so you can put across your message in the most effective way to produce the best result.

The right diagnosis

The right diagnosis is crucial to success in the medical field. Without it, patients suffer and sometimes die. Diagnosing the state of a patient is an organised and logical process. Diagnosis is more than just gathering information; it is applying that information in a way that brings a successful and wanted outcome.

There needs to be an organised and logical diagnosis of the audience to deliver content which accomplishes the right result. Audience profiling is an indispensable part of the design of a presentation.

Presentations need to fit a specific audience the way a prescription is given to fit a specific diagnosis.

Mixed audiences

Very often you will have a mixed audience with different needs and questions. There is no one simple answer to this scenario. This is very testing as a presenter and you need to ask yourself some serious questions:

1. How many groups do I have in my audience exactly?
2. Do I want or need to talk to them all?
3. I cannot talk to them all at the same time so in order of importance who should I talk to first, second and third?

You cannot talk to a mixed audience with different needs at the same time in your presentation. You can address a mixed audience one at a time in the same presentation.

Please remember the only reason an audience listens to you is if they are interested, there is a benefit or they are afraid not to. You must accept that if your presentation is not relevant to a section of the audience they will switch off.

What follows on the next page is a simple one-page template to profile your audience.

You need to write this out in full as the first step to preparing a great presentation. Please note, it is not enough to just think through the template questions in your head, you must actually fill out the template in full.

Until this page is complete you cannot move on to step 2. If the answers are not immediately available you may need to do some research to gain some insight into your audience.

If you have a mixed audience you will need to profile each section of the audience, i.e. you will need to fill out this template for each audience sector.

Audience profiling template

Task 1	Who is in my audience for this presentation?
1.	
2.	
3.	

If there is a mixed audience in the room, who is the group I want to influence most? Is there a second or third group I wish to speak to?

Task 2	Before I present, what does my chosen audience know, think and feel about my presentation topic?
Know:	
Think:	
Feel:	

If my chosen audience members had three questions they wanted answered in my presentation, what would they be and in what order would they want them answered?

Task 3	After I finish my presentation what are the three messages I want my audience to take away and remember?
1.	
2.	
3.	

APPROACH STEP 2 Structuring and shaping your messages

The mark of a great presenter is not what they say, but what they choose not to *say*.

Would you like a piece of chocolate cake?

I want you to imagine you're at a party and you have just been told they are about to serve chocolate cake. You like chocolate cake. You would *love* a piece of the chocolate cake.

Next thing the hostess appears with the chocolate cake on a dirty plate. She then starts using her bare hands to break off pieces of the cake. She then places the mashed-up piece of cake on a piece of toilet paper and hands it to you.

Would you still want the chocolate cake?

Now imagine the hostess wheeled the cake out on a silver cart. She then divides it into perfect slices. She serves it on a china plate and unexpectedly also gives you a glass of champagne.

Now how would you feel about accepting the chocolate cake?

The cake is still the same cake. The way the hostess presents the cake to you is the difference between you wanting it or rejecting it.

The way you introduce, structure and deliver your content in a presentation is what makes an audience accept it or not. Every day I see businesspeople serve an audience unprepared, unplanned, unrehearsed, mashed-up content on ad hoc PowerPoint slides.

The worst part is the audience that would easily accept the information, if served as it should be, is left with no choice but to reject it.

This outcome leaves both the presenter and the audience feeling disappointed, frustrated and ultimately unfulfilled.

What follows over the next few pages is the structure template along with an explanation of how it works to allow you to structure and shape your messages.

Structure template

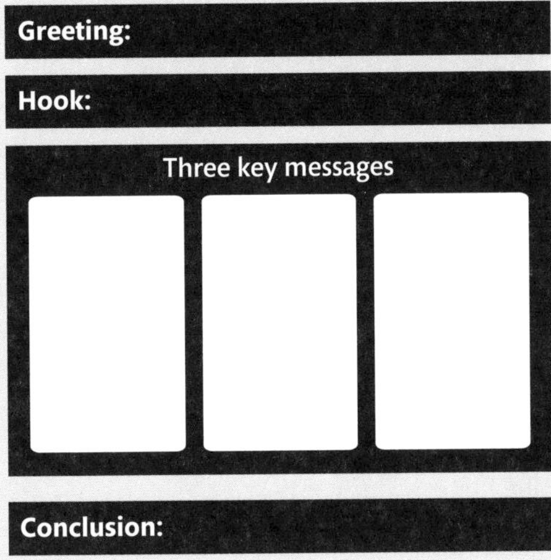

Structure

You have four areas to complete for structuring and shaping your messages:

1. Greeting
2. Hook
3. Three key messages
4. Conclusion

1. Greeting – decide how you will greet the audience

Things to think about when deciding how to greet your audience:

- Does your audience know you?
- Do you have a relationship with them?
- Is it morning or afternoon?
- Are you the first or last to present?

There is no *right way* to greet an audience. Your greeting must be genuine, real and short as this is eating into your 45 seconds.

2. Hook

Earlier in the book we explored the reason an audience will listen and also the need to engage with them in the first 45 seconds. This is what is called the hook.

Many people ask me whether they should tell a joke in the beginning or do something uncanny to grab attention. But the hook is not about tricks. The hook is very simply answering the number one question the audience has which is:

'Why should I listen and what's in it for me?'

3. Three key messages

Before you begin preparing for any presentation all you will have is data. What you need to do as a presenter in preparing for your talk is:

- analyse and edit that data so it is tailored to the audience you are talking to;
- package or group that data into a format that is really easy for you and your audience to understand and follow.

Please be clear, I am not asking you to exclude any important information. I just want you to give it to the audience in a way that is digestible.

You need to divide your data into three core areas or messages. How do you do this? There are a few simple ways:

- Task 2 of the audience profile template asks you to identify the three questions your chosen audience wants answered.
- Task 3 of the audience profile template will give you the three messages you want them to understand.
- Another option is to simply ask your audience in advance of your presentation what three areas it would be of most benefit to cover.

4. Conclusion

Finally, your conclusion is an important part of your talk.

You have hooked the audience and have given them three understandable and clear messages. Now you just want to remind them of the value of your presentation (the same as the hook), thank them and open the floor to questions.

Applying the structure to different presentations

Every single presentation is different because every single audience is different. What follows are four examples of presentation types and how they might fit into the structure I have just explained.

Presenting to inform/educate

This is an example of giving a presentation about the results of a survey that was carried out:

HOOK: Overall the survey results are good news despite a few challenges we may be facing in the future.		
Good news - what's working	Bad news - challenges	Other data that may be of interest to you from the findings
CONCLUSION: As we said this is good news and we plan to draw up a plan in the coming weeks to address the challenges, which we see being resolved in the next three months.		

Presenting to influence/persuade

This is a presentation with the purpose of influencing a team to buy into a new way of doing things:

HOOK: If we don't put this application and approach into place our entire operation will be slowed down and the customer will suffer.		
What is this new application and approach?	How do we implement it and how much will it cost?	What are the obstacles we face implementing this and how do we overcome them?
CONCLUSION: This application is vital for the future success of our business. It must be implemented and to do so the next step is to set up a team to implement and take ownership of it.		

Presenting to motivate/ignite

This is an example of a presentation designed to inspire action based on new legislation that will affect consultancy firms around the globe:

HOOK: There is new legislation coming in 2014 that will affect us and create big opportunities for us, but we need to take action now! I am suggesting three actions.		
Examine our current client base and how this affects them	Come up with individual client action lists	Work together as a firm to utilise every opportunity
CONCLUSION: There are big opportunities for us but we must act now!		

Presenting to sell

Finally, this is a presentation structure that may work when pitching for new business:

HOOK: We understand your business and your challenges and can solve your problem in the most effective way possible.		
We understand you and your problem	We have a tried and tested solution we can offer you	We are the right company for you to work with
CONCLUSION: We understand your business and your challenges and can solve your problem in the most effective way possible.		

Shaping your messages – the 3 × 3 rule

At this stage you have the framework for a great presentation. You have a hook, three key messages and a conclusion.

The next step is to decide what you are going to say under each message. This is where you decide on the rest of the content of your presentation. Different audiences will need different information. What you are trying to do here is pick the most relevant and interesting information to back up your key messages for your chosen audience.

The final message structure should follow the 3 × 3 rule:

Three clear core messages explained and expanded on with the three most compelling and impactful pieces of information you have to support each message.

Please note you don't have to have exactly the full 3 × 3 in every presentation. You can have less. This is, however, the maximum I recommend for a business presentation.

This structure ensures you don't mix up your messages. Message 1 is explained and delivered, then you move onto message 2 and then finally you address message 3. With this structure you have a very clear beginning, middle and end to your presentation.

Message 1	Message 2	Message 3
1st piece of info	1st piece of info	1st piece of info
2nd piece of info	2nd piece of info	2nd piece of info
3rd piece of info	3rd piece of info	3rd piece of info

Shaping your messages: three steps

To figure out what the three most compelling and understandable pieces of information are that will support your overarching message you must do three things:

1. A data dump.
2. Explore all the ways you can tell your story.
3. Take out the trivial.

Step 1: Do a data dump

With each separate message begin by using the mind map tool below and brainstorm all the possible things you could say about your message. Get everything out of your head and onto paper.

Step 2: Explore all the ways you can tell your story

Again, taking each message separately you **now** explore all the different ways you can make your message engaging and understandable.

To do this you need to answer the eight questions that follow as best you can. (You may not be able to answer all of them as they may not all be relevant for each message.)

1. What is the definition for this message?
2. What is the technical explanation for this message?
3. What is the one-sentence explanation of the message?
4. If you had to explain this message to a lay person, what would you say?
5. Can you give an example to explain this message?
6. Can you give a case study to explain this message?
7. Can you give an analogy to explain this message?

8. Is there any other relevant information that would add value to this for the audience?

Step 3: Take out the trivial

Now it's time to apply the MoSCoW principle (a business prioritisation method) to your data dump and the answers to your eight questions. Prioritise all your information into:

- **M**ust have
- **S**hould have
- **C**ould have
- **W**on't have

If you are still having trouble deciding what to leave in and what to take out of your messages, apply the 'So what?' principle.

Just imagine your audience saying 'So what?' at the end of everything you are proposing to say.

It should now be clear what are the three most compelling and impactful pieces of information you have written down to support your messages.

Recap

For each message, 1, 2 and 3, simply repeat the steps.

1. Use the mind map tool to data dump all the information that might be worth including in your message.
2. Answer the eight questions that help you generate a clearer explanation of your message.
3. Then apply the MoSCoW principle.
4. Finally, if all else fails, ask the 'So what?' question.

APPROACH STEP 3
Design your visual aids

Would your audience rather go to the dentist than listen to you?

As a member of an audience watching a presentation do you like it when the presenter has lots of text on their slides? I ask this question on a daily basis and I always get the same answer: *'No, I don't like text-heavy slides as an audience member.'*

A recent survey has not only confirmed this finding but has gone one step further, concluding that we would rather do a multitude of mundane or self-sacrificing activities than sit through a presentation with text-heavy slides.

- 24 per cent of people would rather forgo a night of sex.
- 21 per cent would rather do their taxes.
- 20 per cent would rather go to the dentist.
- 18 per cent would rather work on Saturdays.

According to the survey carried out by SlideRocket the top frustration and guaranteed way to turn an audience off is by having slides with too much text. These types of presentations have put 24 per cent of people to sleep and 30 per cent of an audience have actually left the room during the talk.

The big three

1. **Prezi** is a cloud-based storytelling tool for exploring and sharing ideas on a virtual canvas.
2. **PowerPoint** is a presentation software program that uses a graphical approach to presentations in the form of slide shows that accompany the oral delivery of the topic.

3. **Keynote** is Apple's own presentation application that allows you to create presentations on your Mac and access them on your iPad, iPhone or iPod Touch.

Let me begin by saying I have no preference when it comes to slideware. To me PowerPoint, Keynote and Prezi are all tools to build slides. They are slide-centric, rather than message-centric.

However, 99 per cent of the people I work with use PowerPoint so I am going to draw on that as my basis for talking about slides. Please note any point I make about PowerPoint relates or can be adapted to the other presentation software.

The message I want to deliver to you in this section is that a presentation is not about the slides, it is about you presenting a great, clear message, slides or no slides.

> **If I took your Prezi, Keynote or PowerPoint slides off you, could you deliver your presentation without them?**

We do not walk around in everyday life accompanied by slides. Imagine going to a party and plodding through a PowerPoint to talk about your week. Going home to your partner and whizzing through a Prezi as you talk about your day. Lunch with your friends would not be same if you had to keep in line with your Keynote talk.

Using slides in a presentation is an *option*.

You don't have to use slides

If you prepare a great message the option to use slides or not use slides is just that, an option. They do not become a must, they become a 'would be good to have for the audience to understand the message better'.

One of the big issues with slideware is people spend more time picking animations then profiling their audience, and pay more attention to sound effects than structure.

It isn't which software you use that is important, but how you use it. The important part is what goes on before you prepare the slides. You are going to have to experiment with the software yourself to decide what you like, but whatever your preference you must take the three-step approach before you go near your PowerPoint, Prezi or Keynote:

1. **Profile your audience**
2. **Structure and shape your messages**
3. **Design visual aids**

Then you can use any software you like.

I am not here to debate the pros and cons of PowerPoint, Keynote or Prezi. This is a whole other book in itself. I am here to challenge you to ask yourself one very simple question:

Are you
missing the
point of
PowerPoint
?

Overleaf is a sample of the slides I see every day.

Presentation slides are being over-used and abused. People give the following reasons for over-using and exploiting slideware:

- 'Everyone else's slides looks like this.'
- 'They were used by the last speaker therefore I have to use each and every one of them!'
- 'If I don't use them people will think I have not prepared properly.'
- 'They help me remember what to say next.'
- 'The audience will be more interested if there are words they can read.'
- 'If I miss a point the audience can read it on the slides.'
- 'People will think I'm more professional.'

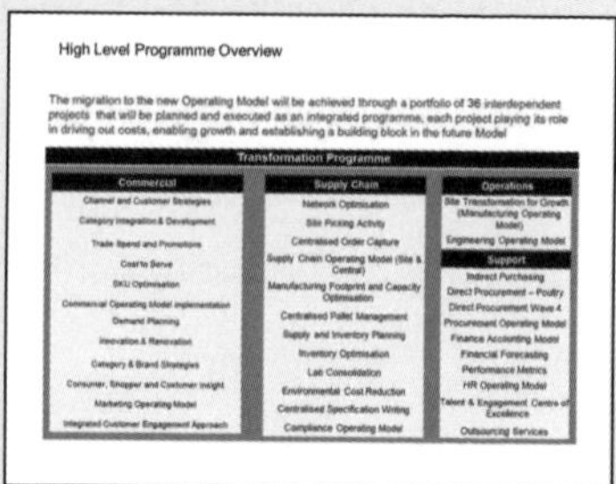

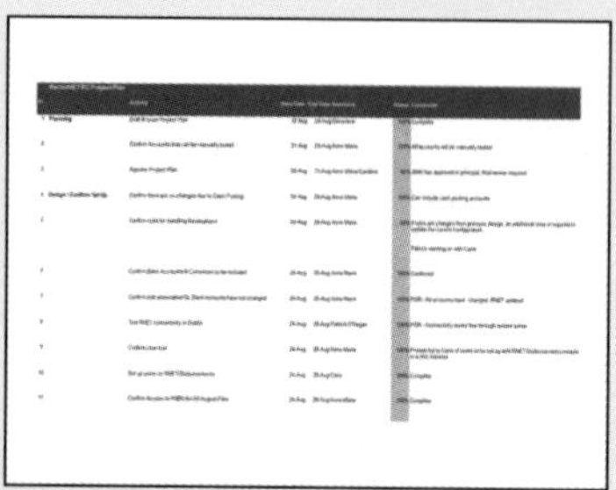

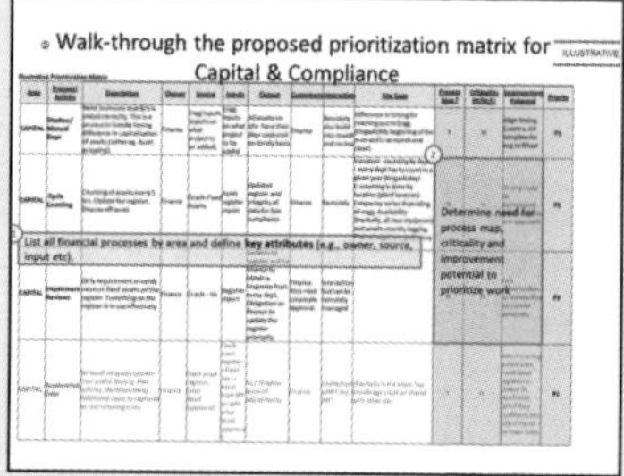

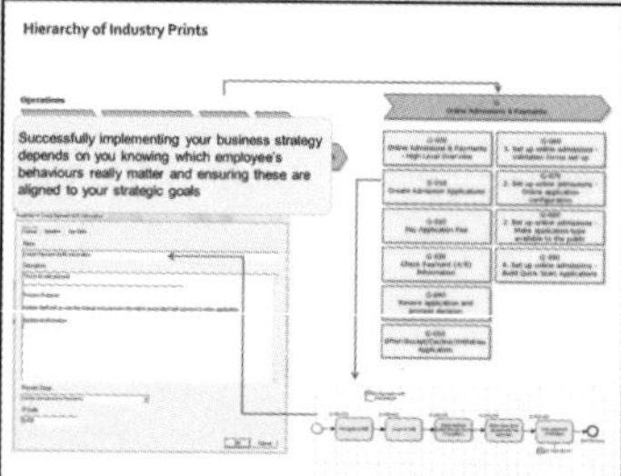

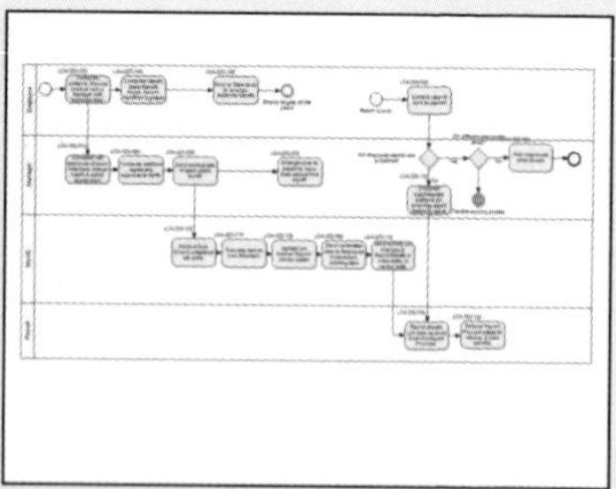

The point of PowerPoint

The slides are not for you, they are for the audience. Slides are a visual aid to help the audience understand and remember your messages. You build your slides around your talk and not the other way around. Your slides should be very simple and relevant.

What follows are my top ten tips for putting the power into your PowerPoint. I have also asked my slide designer Ed to give you some insight into slide design before you look at designing your own.

1. PREPARING SLIDES IS THE LAST THING YOU DO

You must profile your audience, structure and shape your messages and then work on how to make your messages visual. You design your slides around your messages.

Do not start here!

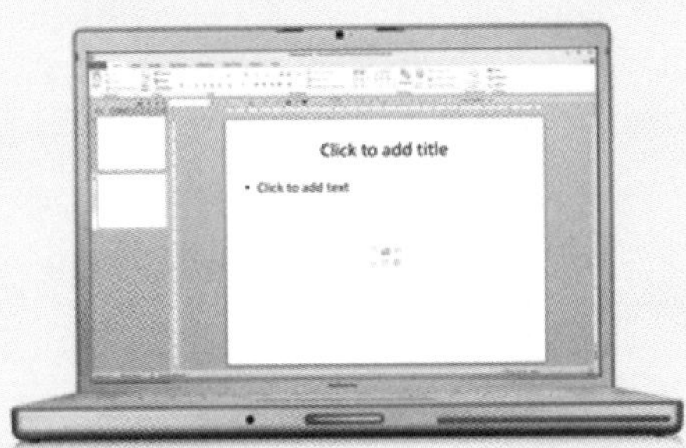

2. A VISUAL AID (SLIDE) AND A HANDOUT ARE TWO COMPLETELY DIFFERENT PIECES OF COMMUNICATION WITH TWO COMPLETELY DIFFERENT PURPOSES

The slide is supposed to complement what you say, not act as a distraction. The handout is what the people in the room are meant to take away and refer to after the presentation, when you are no longer there to wow them with your brilliant presentation skills and charm.

Slide

Getting your message across

- Research has shown that it is of great importance to grab people's attention as quickly as possible.
- Research has shown that the ideal time for this appears to be within the first 45 seconds of a presentation.

Handout

If you give an audience a handout before your talk or put all the text from the handout on the slide the audience will read ahead and not listen to you. If that is happening then what is the point in you being there?

3. DO NOT USE A PICTURE FOR THE SAKE OF IT

I was working with a group in a law firm telling them their presentations should be visual.

The next day, I got a phone call from my client to say this group stood up to present and had random pictures of judges and legal scales all over their presentations. When they were asked why, they said, 'Emma told us to use pictures!'

I did not tell them to use pictures, I told them to use visuals. A visual is an image that helps make your message easier to understand. Your image has to have meaning. No random judges allowed!

4. OK PEOPLE, IT IS ONE MESSAGE PER SLIDE AND ONE MESSAGE ONLY

The audience should look at your slides and have an 'Aha' moment. Your slides are supposed to create clarity. Your audience are not supposed to have to squint, have speed-reading abilities or have to frantically search through the spreadsheet on the slide to find the number you are referring to when you say 'as you can see from this slide'.

One message per slide is the rule.

It doesn't matter if you have 20 slides or two slides. They are just for you to speak with. The handout, of course, does not have to follow this rule as it is a written document so you can go crazy with the number of messages per page on that.

5. FIVE WORDS ACROSS, FIVE WORDS DOWN

I know some of you are freaking out right now wondering are you allowed to use any text on your slides at all? Of course you are, but there is a rule about how much text is appropriate and you need to stick to it: you can have **five words across** and **five words down**.

Now, I did not say five sentences. There are no sentences allowed on a visual slide. It is PowerPoint … point. You the presenter are the full sentence. You are the text. You are the presentation. That is why you are there.

Talk to the audience and stop making the slides do your work. The slide just shows the key points. If you have more than five across and five down you need two separate slides.

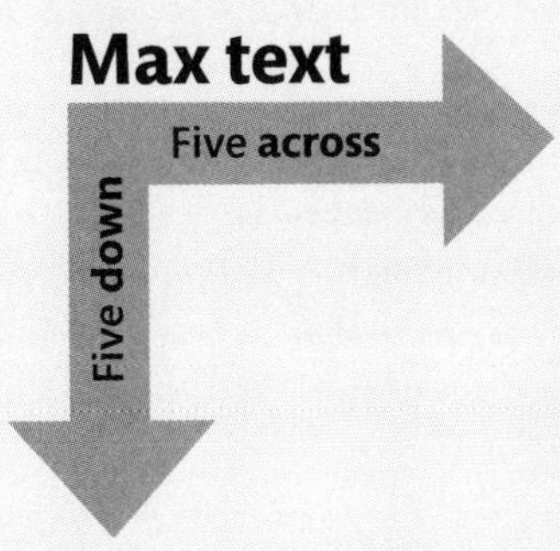

6. ANIMATING TEXT

Animating text means that each bulleted point of your slide appears on the screen one at a time. For example, if you are going to have five words across and five down then you need to animate them so they appear on the screen one by one. If you put all five up together then you will be talking about point number one and your audience will be … well you have no idea where they will be. Point 2, point 3, point 5, wishing you would hurry the hell up because this is time they are never getting back.

Building text

- **One point appears**

Building text

- **One point appears**
- **Then the next**

Building text

- **One point appears**
- **Then the next**
- **Then the next**

7. TRANSITIONING BETWEEN SLIDES

When you are moving from one slide to another there are many fancy ways you can do this – it is called slide transitioning. Each presentation software has its own version of this and below are examples of nine possible ways to do it in PowerPoint.

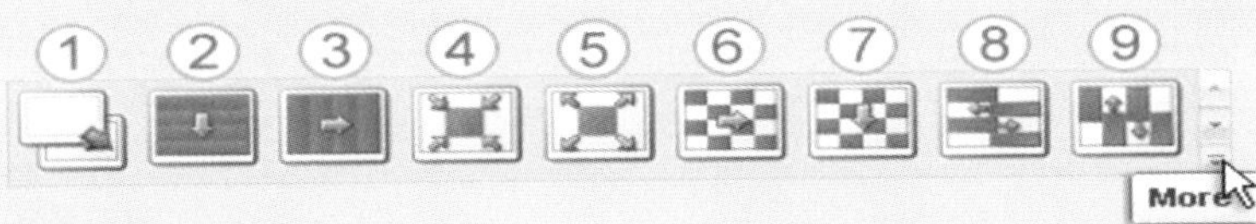

1. No transition
2. Blinds horizontal
3. Blinds vertical
4. Box in
5. Box out
6. Checkerboard across
7. Checkerboard down
8. Comb horizontal
9. Comb vertical

You are allowed to use **just one** slide transition type in each presentation.

So for the people who use all nine in one presentation (I've seen you) you need to stop showing off. It is disorientating, you are giving your audience motion sickness, and nine transitions does not a good presentation make.

8. THE PRESENTER LEADS THE SLIDES NOT THE OTHER WAY AROUND

This is what most people do when operating their slides:

1. They click onto the slide.
2. They pause and have a look at the slide to get a prompt. This pause is possibly accompanied by a look of shock (did I put that slide there?), an expression of fear (what am I going to say about this?) or an air of apathy (could this talk be any more boring?).
3. They then start talking about whatever point is on the slide.

They repeat this for the entire presentation.

This is not how it should be. You the presenter should introduce your slide and tee up what is coming before you click on the slide itself. You are the leader and the slide is the follower. You must introduce your slide before you click on the slide itself.

The presenter leads the slides and not the other way around.

Presenter first
Slide second

How do you get to the point where you can do this? There is only one way: preparation.

9. THE SCREEN IS NOT FOR YOU

The people in the audience have taken the time to come and hear your presentation so the least you can do is look at them and not turn your back and talk to the slides.

Yes, maybe they have been forced to come and listen to you but either way you have more chance of actually engaging them if you turn around and look at them.

But how will you see your slides? You are going to put a laptop in front of you with the slides on it (and your notes if you need to) and you are going to use this to see the same slides the audience can see.

The laptop is for you, the screen is for the audience. You must stand with your back to the screen and your hips facing the audience at all times.

If you need to point something out on the screen you step back in line with the screen and you turn your head and your arm to point. You do not turn your back on the audience at any time during a presentation. Ever.

The screen is not for you

Make eye contact

10. B AND W

This is just a little trick I thought you might find useful. When your slide show is on full view if you press B or W the screen will turn to black or white respectively. If you hit B or W again it will come back to the same slide.

This is really powerful if you want to blank the screen, grab the audience's attention and make a point.

GETTING YOUR SLIDES RIGHT
Ed Fidgeon-Kavanagh of Clearpreso.com

Your slides are your opportunity to bring your presentation to life in a visual way. These slides are fully intended for your audience, not for you as a script. In fact, reading your slides out word for word is about as surefire a way to lose your audience as I can imagine. So here are a few tips to help you on your way to creating better slide decks.

Don't start at the computer

Before you even go near a computer, it's a good idea to sketch out your ideas on what you would like your slides to communicate on paper. You could do this in a notebook, or on sticky notes, the important thing is that you don't immediately get into the 'PowerPoint' mindset.

Don't worry about slide count

Despite what others might say, in my opinion there is no 'ideal number' when it comes to slides. You should use as many slides as it takes to tell your message in a natural, flowing manner. For example, rather than cramming three graphs on one slide to meet some arbitrary slide count, spread them out over three slides. The amount of information is exactly the same – being concerned with artificially condensing it onto one slide is counter-productive. If you tell an interesting story, and make sure the information flows well, people will not know, or care, how many slides you have used.

Keep it visual

Where possible try to create slides that use supporting imagery. We are better at remembering and recalling points when they are mixed with images, it helps it seem more real. Why not even use some of your own imagery? If you are talking about 'My Team' use a real photo of yourselves. The more real you can make your information the better. For high quality images check out one of the many stock photography websites out there. My personal favourite is canstockphoto.com.

Keep it simple

The message must be given absolute priority over everything else. You do not need a logo and tagline on every slide – they aren't helping people understand your message. You do not need a complex, overly busy template, it is all noise with no signal. What you need is clarity, and with that in mind I suggest you strip out anything that is not helping you get your message across.

Inspiration is all around you

In your day-to-day life you will come across great examples of visual communication. Posters, magazines, books and even street signs have important design features that you can learn from, so always keep an eye open for examples of communication that you can emulate in your presentation.

Design your visual aids

You need to begin the process of creating your visuals away from the computer. A great way to do this is to start with a storyboard, on paper. Overleaf is a template that you can use to storyboard your visuals. A good alternative to this is to use sticky notes and arrange them on your desk or the nearest wall you can find.

You need to look at your structure and ask yourself how you can make each message visual or more understandable.

Once you have them designed and in the right order on paper, you can create the real ones on presentation software.

Sticky notes will help keep your message clear and concise.

Storyboard template

Chapter 8

Going live

Delivery

A presentation is made up of two parts: **communication** and **delivery**.

Up to now we have been looking at communication and the approach to structure and shape your messages. I would now like to address delivery skills. These are the skills needed when you're standing in front of the audience. If you do all the preparation we have looked at up to now then a lot of what I am going to talk about will happen naturally because you will own your messages. However, there are a number of things you must be aware of and in some cases manage when you stand up in front of an audience.

Performance

The part of a presentation where you stand up and speak, your presentation delivery, is a performance.

A lot of people don't like it when I say that to them. They recoil in disgust, believing I am now asking them to do something that goes against their nature.

When I talk about a performance, I don't mean an act. You don't need to be someone else. I don't mean something false or fake. You don't need to pretend to be something you're not.

What I mean by a performance is you need to be in a great mood when you present. You need to be the best version of yourself when you present. You need to bring energy and enthusiasm to the presentation.

You can't just go through the motions when you present

Here are the things you need to consider and master for your delivery style to complement your communication.

PERFORMANCE

Passion, humour, energy and personal style
Eye contact
Root yourself to the ground
Filler words
One at a time
Rehearsal
My hands
Anxiety
Notes
Confidence
Expect the unexpected

Passion, humour, energy and personal style

Passion

Passion is an essential ingredient for your delivery skills to be impactful.

Passion simply means you care about what you are talking about, your subject, your audience, getting the right result or simply being a great presenter.

Passion is the opposite of indifference. If you feel your presentation/ content is boring and irrelevant then this is how you are going to make the audience feel. I know some content is easier to get excited about than others but the truth is all data is boring and dry in its rawest form. A great presenter brings it to life. If you are not engaged in your own topic then you need to find a way to get engaged. Change the content around and get some great examples and stories. Find the value in your messages from the audience's point of view. Find a way to make your content enjoyable and digestible.

Unfortunately, passion is not a skill. It is not something I can teach you. If you hate your job or you think what you do is boring then a book on presentation skills is not what you need. A new job is what you need.

Humour

I cannot give you passion and I cannot make you funny, sorry. I get asked a lot by budding presenters if they should tell a joke or be funny. My reply is to ask them whether they have the gift of being able to make people laugh.

There is nothing more cringe-worthy than someone trying to be funny - either you are or you aren't.

You do not need to be a comedian to deliver a great presentation.

What you do need is to bring your data to life by telling stories and using your experience and personality to make the presentation enjoyable.

Focusing on being funny is going to stop you being yourself. Be yourself and trust your own style.

Energy

OK, you like your job. You enjoy talking about numbers. You see the value in your processes. You get excited about your service.

But here's the thing. You got two hours sleep, had a fight with your partner, your most valued client is unhappy, and your deadline has just been moved to a time sooner than you're ready for. On top of that you now have to deliver a presentation and perform.

'Are you kidding me, Emma?' I hear you cry.

I am not kidding and it is not easy to perform when you have a life going on around you. What you must do is *leave it at the door.*

I was told about this when I worked for MTV and I rejected the concept at first. I found it very challenging to leave my life at the door, forget my frustrations and worries, and perform. That felt false to me.

It took me a while to understand that my audience had no interest in what was going on in my life. I couldn't bring that into a TV studio and today I can't bring that into a training room. If I do, it may not be obviously visible but it will be present in everything I do and say and the audience will be able to feel it.

I have to leave it at the door and find a way to be in the room and in a good mood. I need to get my head in a good place before I begin presenting.

I have two strategies to help me do this. I listen to music (I have a specially prepared playlist) or I go and have a few minutes to myself before I talk to clear my head.

You set the mood and tone of the room as a presenter. Your audience deserve the best version of you no matter what is going on in your world.

Personal style

You are the presentation and you are unique. Everyone has a different delivery style and there is no one style or personality that wins over another. Your personal style comes across in the way you dress and behave, in your voice and in the way you tell your story.

You are a walking, talking personal brand. The only thing you need to consider is what you want your brand or personal style to say about you.

WHAT ARE YOU FAMOUS FOR?

I regularly work with students still in college. They are approximately 20 years old. I always talk to them about personal branding and building a successful long-term career. I ask them what impression they want to leave with the audience after they have presented. This is what they tell me:

- 'I want to be funny' – this is always the response from the guys in the room.
- 'I want to be nice and friendly' – this is what the girls in the room hope to be known for.

I picture these individuals 10 years down the road wondering why they are not succeeding as much as they would like. If their goal is to be nice, then that is what they will achieve. If being funny is what is important then this is the impression they will leave. Although it will be unconscious, every time they interact with an audience this is the impression they will leave. Is that a bad thing?

Let's imagine their first employer, with hundreds of graduates to choose from and only a small amount of positions available. They have their pick of the bunch.

What is the employer looking for? Someone who is confident, professional, prepared, a good presenter. These are the attributes my interns should have been aiming for. Yes, be fun and, of course, be nice but not on its own. Be fun, nice, confident and a great presenter.

I tell you this because I want you to ask yourself what impression you want to leave after you present. Are you trying to be nice or funny or is your goal to be impactful and engaging? You will be whatever you set your mind to. The choice is yours.

Eye contact

Eye contact is how we build relationships. It is how we build trust and credibility. We are always suspicious of someone who doesn't make eye contact with us. When you are presenting you must make meaningful eye contact with the audience.

This is sometimes easier said than done because audiences have a way of being very distracting when you look at them during a presentation.

There are four reasons why people fail to make eye contact:

1. **Denial**: The belief that 'if I don't look at the audience and don't see them looking at me then maybe they are not really there'. They are there, they do see you and you do need to look at them.
2. **The slides are the presentation**: This is the presenter who actually turns their body away from the audience and talks to their slides for the entire presentation. (Please see point number 1: your audience is there, they do see you and you need to look at them.)
3. **Anywhere but the eyes**: Instead of meaningful eye contact a presenter will pick a spot at the back of the room to stare at or will look at their audience's foreheads and not their eyes. Please don't do this. It is daft and the audience can see you!
4. **It's the audience's fault**: Audiences have a way of being very distracting when you look at them. They move, they cross their arms, they check their phones, they frown, they talk, they look confused, they seem annoyed, they appear bored, they remain silent and most annoying of all they are sitting there judging you. With all this in mind it is no wonder it is an undertaking just to look at them. Nevertheless they deserve proper eye contact.

You need to look at the audience. This is how you do it.

Be a lighthouse!

You must stand with your entire body facing the audience. You need to make eye contact as if you are a lighthouse. You must ensure you are sweeping around the group slowly moving from left to right or right to left. As you sweep you must engage with each person for roughly two seconds.

Be careful to really look at each person so that they know you're interested in each one of them. Do not look at any one person for too long or they will feel uncomfortable. This applies to both small and large groups. However, in a large group you may not be able to look at each and every person, but ensure you are sweeping across all areas of the general group.

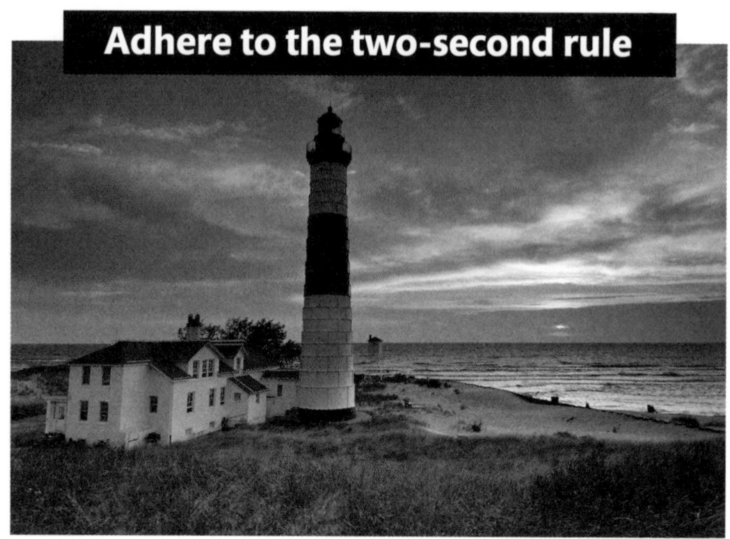
Adhere to the two-second rule

Root yourself to the ground – my one body-language rule

There are entire books written about body language and the nuances of non-verbal communication. I have just one very simple thing to say to you about body language.

> **Don't let your body language take away from your messages.**

Your audience are not supposed to be leaving a room talking about your body language.

- If your body language is good the audience won't even notice it. That is how it should be.
- If your body language is ineffective it is all your audience will talk about and take away from your presentation.

I live by one very simple rule when it comes to body language. Don't let it be a distraction for the audience.

Distracting body language behaviours look like this:

- The presenter dances around, taps toes, or rocks back and forth.
- The presenter sways hips from side to side or constantly shifts weight from one foot to the other.
- The presenter moves around the room with no purpose.

Body language best practice:

- The presenter should stand with feet shoulder width apart, toes pointed forward, with weight distributed equally on each foot - almost as if feet were in a block of cement. The hips of the presenter should be facing the audience at all times. This is what is called being rooted to the ground.
- When a presenter moves, it should be with purpose (e.g. to go to the flipchart, to move to the other side of the room, to walk into the group to make a point). Once the presenter has arrived at the destination, he/she becomes rooted.

Filler words – banish your ums and ahs

Um … Eh … I think … I suppose!

Filler words are … eh … I suppose … words that find their way … um … into our presentations and … eh … I think … most presenters don't want to say them but they … I suppose … don't really know how to stop!

Your filler words, sounds and phrases are actually pot holes in your presentation road for the audience. Every time you use a filler word the audience experiences a bump and discomfort. Too many bumps and your audience will leave the talk feeling a little bruised and battered.

One of the most common challenges I come across on a daily basis in my training courses is the use of filler words. People know they are doing it but can't seem to stop it. There are some really common filler sounds, words and phrases used by most people such as:

- filler sounds – e.g. um, uh, ah, mm;
- filler words – e.g. basically, actually, like;
- filler phrases – e.g. 'I think', 'you know', 'I suppose'.

So what exactly are filler words?

Filler words represent a verbal hesitation that has to be filtered out by your audience. Repeated and excessive use of filler words weakens your credibility. It may be perceived as indicating lack of preparation, lack of knowledge, or lack of passion.

You can most easily identify a filler word if it's a part of the presentation that is said but never written. It's often an irrelevant transitory word used to give yourself more time to find the right word you're looking for, gather your complete thought or idea, and finally finish your sentence.

So why do we fill our presentations with words that add no value and in fact detract from both our message and our overall impact?

There are three main reasons for the use of filler words:

1. We are thinking as we are talking live in front of an audience. We are thinking about what comes next because we haven't quite figured it out yet. The reason is a lack of proper preparation and rehearsal.
2. We are afraid of silence. When you are presenting, a three-second pause can feel like three hours and rather than feel the discomfort a presenter fills every second with a sound.
3. We really are not sure what we are talking about so our filler words reflect the real amount of understanding we have about our topic – i.e. not enough.

So how do you overcome these challenges?

1. The first step is awareness. You must become aware of what filler words you are using and then identify from the list above why you think you are using them.
2. The most simple and effective way to reduce and even eliminate filler words is to practise out loud a minimum of three times before you present for real. This way you will have done your thinking and found your flow.
3. Replace the filler word with a pause. You must plan to pause at key points in your presentation either before or after you deliver an important message. A pause is when you stop, breathe in and breathe out. It lasts between two to three seconds. It will take time to get used to the silence but persevere.
4. You must understand and get to grips with your own topic before you can communicate it to someone else. If you are not sure of your message no one else in the room is going to get clarity.

One point at a time – planning to pause

We talked earlier in the book about self-survival. When you are standing in front of an audience it is natural to want to talk through your presentation as quickly as possible and sit back down again. The faster you get it over with the less chance there is of things going wrong. Also that awful audience is still judging you so the quicker the experience is over the better.

On top of that you probably have lots of data to get through so you have to talk fast to get through it all, right?

Not anymore. One of the most important delivery tools you need as a presenter is the pause.

> **A pause is when you stop talking, you take a breath in and then a breath out.**

As I mentioned when I was addressing filler words, it lasts about three seconds. Those three seconds will feel like three hours. The silence in the room can be very overwhelming for any presenter (hence the enormous urge to fill up every single second of the talk with your voice).

You pause:

- for your audience to digest your messages;
- so you, the presenter, can breathe.

You need to embrace, plan and practise your pausing.

Most presenters don't talk too fast, they simply don't allow any space between their key points.

- You need to pause at the beginning of your presentation before you start to make sure the audience is ready to listen.
- You need to pause either before or after you make an important point.
- You need to pause when you put up a slide to allow people to take it in.

Pausing is like an amber traffic light. It slows everything down.

Rehearsal – the secret weapon of great presenting

One of the most overlooked areas in a presentation is the need to rehearse. The truth is in most cases the presenter only realises how vital this step is when they are presenting in front of a real audience and the words won't come, at least not the right ones. Their talk is full of ums and ahs as their brain scrambles desperately under pressure to find a flow between words and points. They take 20 sentences to say what could be said in two because they didn't find the most direct path to their message before they decided to bring their audience there. They didn't rehearse.

OK, so here comes the science …

David Weiner, author of several psychology bestsellers, including the new *Reality Check: What Your Mind Knows But Isn't Telling You*, writes:

> **'Now there's new clinical research that shows there's a physical reason why rehearsing works so well and why those hours of out-loud practice can make you a more confident presenter.'**

Weiner states:

> **'The research shows there are two important reasons why practice makes perfect. The first is that when you practice anything - be it a business, sales or scientific presentation or even Beethoven's "Moonlight" sonata - you essentially carve a path for it in your brain. Without practice, your brain can take any of tens or hundreds of paths to reach its final destination.'**

Practice reduces the number of potential pathways. In other words, by repeating your presentation again and again you'll start using about eight to ten pathways, says Weiner. 'The brain will know what you want it to do,' he says, 'so you'll become more precise.'

A real rehearsal

A real rehearsal is when in advance of your talk you deliver your content with slides, while standing and saying the words out loud in real time without skimming over any detail.

Glancing over your notes or reading through your slides in bed or on some sort of public transport is not a rehearsal.

To ensure your audience are taking the right path you must rehearse **a minimum of three times for any presentation.**

Rehearse three times minimum
Out loud with visuals
× 3

REHEARSAL RULES - SEVEN STEPS TO SUCCESS

1. Rehearse your presentations at least three times.
2. Always rehearse out loud not in your mind.
3. Always rehearse with all your slides and props.
4. Always endeavour to rehearse once at the final location.
5. Check from the back of the room that your visuals can be seen clearly and you can be heard.
6. Arrive before everyone else (a minimum of 30 minutes before).
7. Check all the equipment 24 hours before, bring a back-up and have a plan B.

My hands – what do I do with them?

Picture the scene. I have just delivered a one-hour presentation. I have spent two weeks preparing and rehearsing. I have just discussed my three-step approach in detail.

I have left my negative feelings at the door and I have talked with passion and energy (if I do say so myself). I am exhausted but happy.

I feel I have really got my point across about how a great presentation is about ownership and content crafting. I open the floor to questions. I wait with held breath for feedback from my audience and for a glimmer of insight that shows me my messages have landed. The first question comes: *'Hi Emma, yeah that was great and all, but what do I do with my hands when I present?'*

I am not going to lie. I die a little inside. I jest, because the reality is this is a real concern for millions of people. Like body language, gestures and information on what to do with your hands can take up entire books.

My understanding and practice of what to do with your hands is the same as what to do with your body language.

Don't let your gestures take away from your messages.

Your audience shouldn't be leaving the room talking about your gestures.

- If your hand movements are appropriate the audience won't even notice them. That is how it should be.
- If your gestures are distracting and ineffective it is all your audience will talk about and take away from your presentation. This is not how it should be.

Don't let your hand movements be a distraction for the audience. Distracting hand movements look like this:

- fidgeting of any sort;
- nervous repetitive movements (e.g. touching your face or hair);
- hands on hips or both hands in pockets;
- holding/clicking/ fidgeting with a pen;

- holding/fumbling/fidgeting with your notes.

Gesturing best practice looks like this:

- First and foremost you must be yourself. Some people gesture a lot, some not at all. There is no right or wrong as long as it is not a distraction.
- Become aware of your gestures through feedback or watching yourself on video.
- Place your hands at your sides, unless gesturing or using a visual aid.
- The key is to practice this, and it will eventually feel more comfortable. This is a very confident, open stance.
- Gesture from your shoulder and not from your wrist.

Anxiety – please make the nerves go away

If there is anyone reading this book who can stop me feeling nervous can you please email me immediately? Seriously!

I have been presenting for 18 years and I still get nervous all the time.

Usually my level of nervousness depends on the group in front of me and how intimidating I perceive them to be. I am also one of those people who gets more nervous in front of people I know. I prefer talking to an audience of strangers.

I have always accepted my nerves as part of what I do. The days on television when I felt comfortable were the days I performed the worst so as much as I don't like feeling nervous I reckon my nerves must be doing me some good. I would be worried if I wasn't nervous.

I never focus on my nerves, I never think about my nerves. I know my nerves will be there. I work very hard to ensure that when my nerves are at their worst at the beginning of an important presentation, I have prepared to get me through it.

The only two techniques I have found to help me when I am feeling very nervous and I can't get my mind to quieten down are:

1. Mentally challenging the fear.

2. Mindful breathing.

Here comes the science ...

Anxiety or nervousness is the body's way of responding to being in a life or death situation.

Adrenaline is rushed into our bloodstream to enable us to run away or fight. This happens when the danger is real or when we believe the danger is there when actually there is none. It is the body's alarm and survival mechanism.

This is what happens to people when they present, especially in the few minutes before they are about to speak. What this simply means is your internal survival system cannot tell the difference between a life and death situation and a presentation.

Embarrassing yourself in front of a room full of people is life or death for your ego so that is why the feelings are so strong.

The first step in managing your nerves is recognising this response and why it is happening. Your body is just telling you this is important and you don't want to mess it up.

Thoughts that often occur when you are about to present:

- This is a life or death situation.
- The worst possible scenario is going to happen and I will embarrass myself.
- I won't be able to cope with this and I will make a mess.

PHYSICAL SENSATIONS – THE ADRENALINE RESPONSE

When there is real, or we believe there is a real, threat or danger, our bodies' automatic survival mechanism kicks in very quickly. This helps energise us to fight or run away ('fight or flight response'). The action urge associated with anxiety is to escape or avoid. We will therefore notice lots of physical sensations, which might include:

- **Heart racing:** This helps to take the blood to where it is most needed – the legs so that we can run faster (flight); the arms so that we can hit out (fight); the lungs to increase stamina. At the same time blood is taken from the places it is not needed, for example fingers, toes and skin. These changes cause tingling, coldness and numbness.
- **Breathing gets faster:** This helps the bloodstream to carry oxygen to the arms, legs and lungs. This will give us more power. The side effects may include chest pain, breathlessness and a choking feeling. As there is a slight drop in the blood and oxygen being sent to the brain we may feel dizzy or light-headed, and we may experience blurred vision.
- **Sweating:** This helps to cool the muscles and the body. It helps to stop them from overheating. Sweating can also make us more slippery to our enemies!
- **Digestive system slows down:** This is not important while in danger and so is slowed down for the saved energy to go to where it is most needed. Side effects may include nausea, butterflies and a dry mouth.

Being nervous before a presentation is totally normal.

Behaviours that will happen to you during the presentation:

- self-talk/inner critique;
- fiddling with clothes or hair or jewellery;
- avoiding eye contact with the audience;
- moving from foot to foot;
- talking fast;
- general fidgeting.

You will do a lot of these things to help you cope with anxiety and yet these behaviours will only show an audience your fear.

The vicious cycle of anxiety or nerves

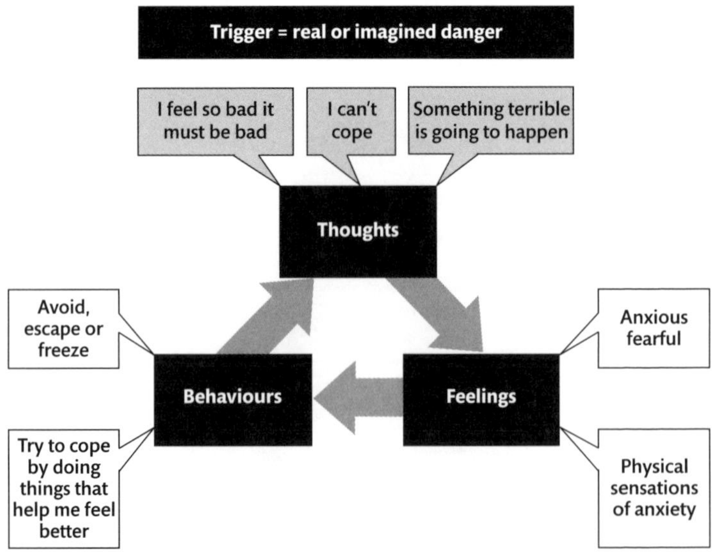

WHAT IS YOUR BELIEF ABOUT PRESENTING?

Negative beliefs make us prone to failing if we try, or may even hold us back from making any effort at all.

It is our limiting beliefs that stop us from reaching our potential. It is the negative voice in our head that repeats to us daily all the reasons we will fail. Negative beliefs are a self-fulfilling prophecy.

Our negative thoughts cause us to behave in a negative way therefore ensuring a negative outcome:

Negative belief = Negative feelings = Negative actions = Reinforced negative belief

With presentation skills the belief cycle goes like this.

The negative belief is:

- 'Presenters are born not made.'
- 'I am not naturally good at this.'
- 'If I stand up, I will make a mess of it.'
- 'I hate presentations. I can't do presentations.'
- 'I don't have time to prepare and anyway people who are good at presenting don't prepare.'

The negative behaviour is:

- no preparation;
- last-minute preparation;
- preparation that is focused on getting the presenter through the talk rather than the audience.

The final result the audience and presenter experience is:

- a nervous unprepared presenter with the wrong focus;
- no engagement with the audience;
- negative feedback.

Because of this result the original belief is reinforced. In order to change the result you must change the belief and you must prepare.

Mentally coping with nerves

STOP! Pause, take a breath, and don't react automatically.

Ask yourself:

- What am I reacting to?
- What is it that I think is going to happen here?
- Is this fact or opinion?
- What's the worst (and best) that could happen? What's most likely to happen?
- Am I getting things out of proportion?
- How important is this really? How important will it be in six months' time?
- Am I overestimating the danger?
- Am I underestimating my ability to cope?
- Am I mind-reading what others might be thinking?
- Is there another way of looking at this?
- What advice would I give someone else in this situation?
- Am I putting more pressure on myself?
- Just because I feel bad doesn't mean things really are bad.

Thinking through the list of questions here can often help you recognise that things are not as threatening as they might seem!

Physically coping with nerves

Practise calming or mindful breathing – this one act alone will help reduce the physical sensations, emotions and intensity of thoughts.

WHAT IS MINDFUL BREATHING?

Imagine your mind when you are nervous as a brand new puppy that you need to toilet train. You allocate an area for the puppy to do his business, you put down some paper and then you show the puppy this area.

What are the chances of the puppy getting it right first time around? None. The puppy will keep wandering to all sorts of other places you don't want him to go and you will have to keep bringing him back to the area with the paper.

This is what it is like trying to calm your mind before you present. Your thoughts will be like the puppy, full of energy about all the possible outcomes and dangers when you present. You have to find a way to keep bringing your mind back to a calm and confident place.

You do this by mindful breathing and it is very simple:

- As you are sitting waiting to present, observe the natural rhythm of the breath. You don't need to force it to be longer, deeper or slower.
- When your mind starts to wander off simply take note of this distraction and bring your attention gently back to your breath.
- If you like, either count up to 10 in-breaths or 10 out-breaths. If you wander off mid-count go back to the start.

Notes - can I use them?

Yes, you can use notes and you should use notes in case you lose your way, which can happen to any presenter. However, you want to use notes in the right way so here are a few things to consider.

- If you are going to use notes use them openly. You don't need to hide them from the audience or pretend you're not using them. Please remember that the audience can see everything you are doing.
- You're allowed to look at your notes. A good time to do this is when you put up a new slide and the audience is getting to grips with the visual. This is also a good time to take a drink of water. Yes, you are allowed to do that too.

- Notes are the outcome of your good preparation. They should be very legible, in a good large font, and have minimal use of sentences – try using one word to remind you of the point you want to make. Your notes are not supposed to look like an essay. If you write your notes like that you will look down during the presentation and not be able to see the wood for the trees.
- Simple cards or A4 sheets of paper are fine for your notes. Never staple the pages of your notes together. It is very distracting when you are moving through them and when you are turning the pages over. It also looks very sloppy. Leave them unstapled and slide them aside once you're finished. Make sure each page is numbered in case you lose the order.
- Your notes should always be in your gaze path. This means placed ahead of you so that your eyes only have to move slightly to look down at them rather than bending your head right down. If you have to look straight down, your head goes down, your voice becomes muffled and all the audience can see is the top of your head.

Confidence – how do I get it?

It is the people with very limited presentation experience who talk to me most about having no confidence. They feel vulnerable and exposed when they present. They feel genuinely shocked they feel this way yet their lack of presentation experience means it is impossible for them to feel anything else.

I feel vulnerable and exposed when I present and I have 18 years of experience. I don't have a magic solution to this. In my mind it is very simple.

To have confidence you must have experience of doing something a lot and belief you can do it without making a fool of yourself (this comes from the experience).

We feel confident about the things in our life we are skilled at. We are skilled at them because we work hard at them and have earned the right to feel confident and competent.

Confidence is not acquired easily and you don't get it for free. There is no shortcut to real confidence. The reasons you don't feel confident as a presenter are:

- you lack the experience (the skill);
- you are not preparing properly or enough (you have not earned the right to feel confident).

Get more experience to build the skill or do more preparation and you will feel more confident.

Expect the unexpected – how to manage questions

'What if I get asked a question I don't know the answer to?'

I believe this is a dread that keeps many a presenter awake at night. What will you do if you are asked a question you don't know the answer to? Let me tell you.

1. This will happen to you. I guarantee it.
2. You do not know everything. I am sorry if this is brand new information to you.
3. You can say you don't know or you can try and bluff an answer (have you ever seen someone bluff an answer ... not a pretty sight). Either way the audience knows you don't know the answer to the question.
4. You must admit you don't know. Explain why you don't know and then tell them you will get back to them with an answer in due course.
5. You must manage your own anxiety around not knowing as you will feel very exposed. (This is not what the audience thinks just what you feel.)

As well as preparing for the presentation you must also prepare for questions. I know you can't foresee 100 per cent of the questions you will be asked but you can certainly predict a number of them based on your audience profile.

In preparing for questions write down:

- the obvious questions you think you will be asked;
- the challenging questions you fear;
- the one question you are most panicked about being asked.

The template opposite will help you prepare for questions. You might want to brainstorm with someone else in case you are too close to your topic and are unable to identify the angles of the audience.

Preparing for questions template

Obvious questions	Challenging questions
1.	1.
2.	2.
3.	3.
4.	4.
5.	5.
6.	6.
7.	7.
8.	8.
9.	9.
10.	10.

What question do I most fear?

Finally, when you are asked a question you can answer confidently, follow this simple method:

- **T**ake the name of the audience member.
- **R**epeat or rephrase the question for the rest of the audience.
- **A**nswer it.
- **C**heck the response to your answer with the audience member.
- **T**hank the audience member.

Chapter 9

Nature versus nurture

Presenting is a skill, it is not a talent, a gift or a gene we are born with.

All too often when I run a course I meet individuals who assert to me that presenting is a talent or a gift rather than a skill like learning to play an instrument, drive a car or play a sport. *'You either have it or you don't!'* they tell me.

These individuals believe the great speakers of our time just stood up and spoke off the cuff dismissing the years of dedication, priority and preparation that has been put in. I assure them that if they were really speaking off the cuff they would certainly not be hailed as the great speakers of our time but rambling, unprepared generalists with no message or impact.

Great presenters are like great musicians or sports people – they work very hard and that is why they are the best.

What does it take to be a master presenter?

A study conducted by psychologist K. Anders Ericsson and two colleagues, with the help of professors at the Berlin Academy of Music, divided student violinists into three groups:

1. Potential to be world-class soloists.

2. Good, but unlikely to succeed professionally.

3. Would become music teachers.

Each violinist was asked the same question, 'Ever since you first picked up the violin, over the course of your entire career, how many hours have you practised?'

Everyone started playing the violin around five years old and during the first few years everyone practised on average two to three hours a week.

At age eight, the amount of practice changed for those who later became the best with the potential to be world-class soloists.

The ones who ended up with the potential to be the best increased their practice time from three hours a week to over 30 hours a week until the age of 20. By this time:

- These elite performers had each accumulated **10,000 hours** of practice.
- The good violin students had totalled **8,000 hours**.
- The future music teachers had totalled only **4,000 hours**.

The same study was done comparing amateur pianists with professional pianists. The amateurs never practised more than three hours a week during childhood and by the age of 20 had totalled 2,000 hours. The professionals increased their practice over time until by the age of 20 they had reached 10,000 hours.

In Ericsson's study there were no 'naturals', musicians who effortlessly floated to the top while practising less than others.

The research suggests that once a musician has enough ability to get into a music school, what distinguishes one performer from another is how hard he or she works. That's it.

> **The people at the top don't work harder or even much harder than everyone else. They work much, much harder.**

The magic formula for presentation success

I was working with one of the world's leading telecommunications companies over a number of years rolling out a series of six-month programmes designed purposefully to up-skill the entire management team and staff in the area of presenting with impact.

The six-month programme involved three distinct phases:

- Phase 1: Participants attend a two-day workshop on presentation skills.
- Phase 2: A one-day follow-up every month for four months involving one-to-one coaching.
- Phase 3: Long-term access to myself and my colleague regarding any specific presentation they are working on.

This was one of the most comprehensive programmes I have been involved in as a trainer. There was substantial investment by the company and a real aspiration to change the presentation culture in this organisation. Everyone on this programme presented as part of their job and had been handpicked by a manager to attend.

What was most interesting was the pattern that emerged over the time I did this work. Without exception participants from each six-month programme fell into one of three categories:

1. The never-to-be-seen-againers
2. There in body
3. The devoted

The never-to-be-seen-againers

They came to the initial course but they didn't prepare or overly engage. They never attended any of the follow-ups. They had no desire to be better presenters and were not willing to put any further work into their presentation skills.

No desire + no commitment = no change

There in body

These guys did attend the two-day course and most (but not all) of the follow-ups. They did have a very real desire to be better presenters, however they did not actually make the changes that were necessary. They turned up each month with the same development needs and despite being given the tools to up-skill they didn't commit to changing their own behaviour. They did the same thing each month hoping for a better result.

Desire - commitment = no change

The devoted

These are the participants who got the results. They had the magic formula. They wanted to be better **and** they put in the work to achieve it. They took all feedback on board and used all the tools in this book consistently until they saw the change they wanted.

So what is the magic formula?

You have to want to be a great presenter and you have to consistently do the right things over and over again until you reach the required level of competence and confidence. It is as simple and as challenging as that.

Desire + commitment = presentation success

Presenting is a skill. You must have the desire to want to be a great presenter and the commitment to learn the skill.

No matter what the skill, be it driving a car, playing a musical instrument or learning to present all human beings go through four stages.

The four stages of learning

The learning process is about making mistakes and learning from those mistakes. However, when we make mistakes as an adult learning to present we judge ourselves harshly for 'not doing it right', 'not being good enough', and we tell ourselves 'that I can never learn this!'

Ironically, not doing it right and making mistakes as you learn to present are vital steps in the learning process to gain this great skill. To become a great presenter you have to go through the four stages of learning as uncovered by Abraham Maslow:

1. **Unconscious incompetence:** 'I don't know that I don't know how to do this.' This is the stage of blissful ignorance before learning begins.
2. **Conscious incompetence:** 'I know that I don't know how to do this.' This is the most difficult stage, where learning begins, and where you will start judging yourself harshly. This is also the stage at which most people give up. Mistakes are integral to the learning process. They're necessary because learning is essentially experimental and experience-based, trial and error. You can only learn by doing and making mistakes. What is very challenging about learning to present is that you are going through this phase in front of an audience that is judging you.
3. **Conscious competence:** 'I know I can do this, I am learning and it is showing.' As you practise more and more you move into the third stage of learning: conscious competence. This feels better, but your presenting still isn't going to be very smooth or fluid, at least not as much as you would like it to be. You will still have to think a lot about your behaviours.
4. **Unconscious competence:** *'I'm a natural!'* The final stage of learning a skill when it has become a natural part of us.

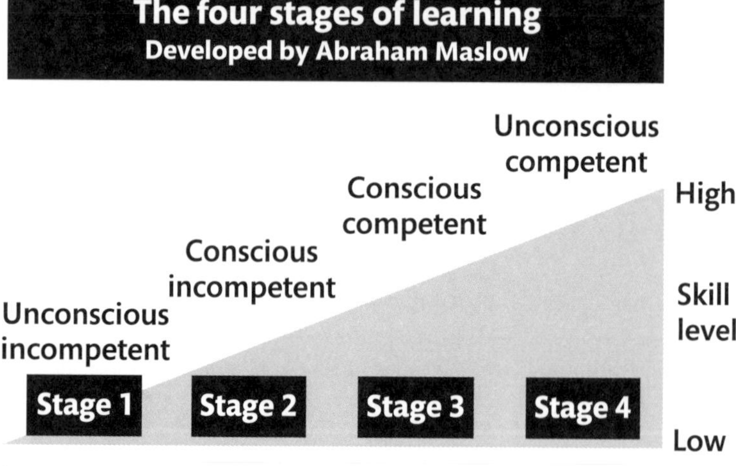

Source: Based on Maslow, A.H. (1943) 'A Theory of Human Motivation', *Psychological Review* 50(4), 370–96. This content is in the public domain.

70/20/10

The 70/20/10 model is a learning and development model based on research by Michael M. Lombardo and Robert W. Eichinger. It states that:

- about 70 per cent of learning comes from direct experience of the skill;
- about 20 per cent of learning comes from feedback from mentors or managers;
- about 10 per cent of learning comes from courses and reading.

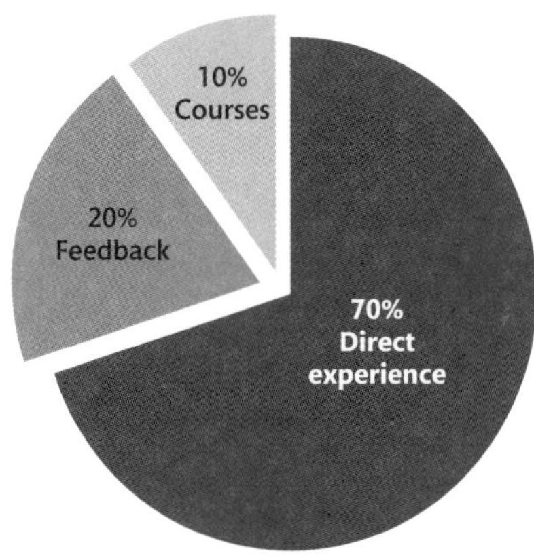

In order for you to develop great presentation skills you must remember these three elements:

1. Present on the job (or wherever possible) on a regular basis.
2. Receive feedback and coaching in line with any training you receive on a continual basis.
3. Understand and gain the skill through attending courses and reading books.

If any of these elements are missing you will not be operating at 100 per cent of your potential.

Your challenge

The skill of presenting can only be gained by presenting. I understand that a difficulty for some of you reading this book is that you have limited opportunity to present in your jobs.

The only way you are going to be able to move through the four stages of learning is to find opportunities to present wherever and whenever you can, in your workplace, by attending a course or by joining a public speaking group in your area.

> **'If nothing changes, nothing changes.'**
>
> EARNIE LARSEN

I keep having the same conversation

It could be a wedding, party (children's or adult), networking event, lunch, breakfast ... hell, any social gathering really and I somehow manage to always get myself into the same debate about my assertion that presenting is a skill that can be acquired.

I do, of course, appreciate and recognise that as with any skill some people take to it more easily than others. Some people enjoy it more than others. Some people want, need and desire to do it more than others.

Is it easier for some people to learn to present? Yes, of course. Do some people have talent? Yes. But talent is not a get out of jail free card. Talent is not a substitute or shortcut for hard work and dedication. If you look at any successful person at the top of their field, even with talent they still work very, very, very hard.

Chapter 10

A reality check

When I work with people I ask them to bring a presentation they have prepared and deliver it for me. I record this presentation on a camera and then I play it back to them.

The question I ask after I record them and before I play it back is, *'Do you think you got your messages across?'*

Most people will be afraid to give any sort of definitive answer and will usually shrug their shoulders and hope for the best. However, in every group there will be someone who says to me with absolute certainty they did get their messages across. They really believe that because they are an expert in their topic or they have been doing their job for so long that they could not fail to get their points across clearly and concisely.

I then usually ask these individuals some questions around what their audience needed and what their audience's level of understanding might be. Again, they assure me they know their audience and what they communicated was hitting the mark.

At this stage I play back the recording.

This individual who believed with conviction they got their messages across clearly appears on screen to be a disconnected speaker who is overloading their audience with unnecessary and untailored information. I can't describe to you the look of shock and feeling of disbelief my participant feels at this moment.

What becomes clear at this point is the lack of self-awareness this person has about their presentation skills. Research conducted by Innermetrix shows the most successful people share the trait of self-awareness.

Great presenters are aware of so many things including – their **audience**, their **content** and **how it is being delivered**. They are aware of their **body language** and how they **interact with the slides**.

How self-aware are you as a presenter?

If I was to ask you to rate your presentation skills, right now, on a scale of 1-10 what number would you give yourself? Imagine 10 is 'I am a master presenter' and 1 is 'I hate it and I am terrible at it'.

The most common ratings I get from my groups are a 5 or 6. Those with more confidence might say 7 or even 8 and those with no confidence rate themselves as low as a 1 or 2. But what is the presentation scale and how do you know exactly where you are on it?

The presentation scale of 1-10 looks like this:

1-4 = very nervous and no presentation skills

A person on the lower end of the scale usually has limited or sometimes no experience on their feet so presenting is terrifying for them. Couple this with a lack of knowledge about what makes a really great presentation and this person is left feeling unsure and incompetent.

5-7 = confident but limited presentation skills

A majority of people I train, especially businesspeople, fall into this category. They do have experience on their feet. They are also what people might call talkers or extroverts.

I recently had a client and I asked him if he thought he was a good presenter. His response was, 'Emma, I come from a family of six, I am well able to talk.' Indeed, he was well able to talk but the reality was he was not presenting well.

If you fall into this part of the scale the good news is you have overcome the hurdle of managing your nerves, which is fantastic. You may feel comfortable and even enjoy presenting. However, what you still don't necessarily have at this stage is the skill to structure and shape a message that is engaging, impactful and meaningful for your audience.

You can present for 20 years and stay at this level. Conference rooms around the globe are filled with presenters who like to talk and have lots of data but never actually get a clear message across.

8–10 = confident and presenting skilfully

When you are truly at this level you have mastered your delivery skills (although you will still get nervous, which is vital) and you will also be capable of crafting a message that always gets the right results. At this level it is about inspiring and leading with your presentations.

How do you know where you really are on this scale?

Your feelings are not an indicator of your abilities. Neither is coming from a family of six! You must examine the components that make up the skill of presenting and objectively measure yourself against them. You must experience yourself as the audience does.

Below is a list of the 12 behaviours you must consistently carry out and demonstrate to be a great presenter.

Assessment of your skill

To get a clearer picture of your skill level please complete the checklist.

When I present:

- I know the purpose of my talk. ☐
- I know the needs of my audience. ☐
- I have prepared clear messages. ☐
- I have structured my messages. ☐
- I have a strong opening and close. ☐
- I use examples and analogies where possible. ☐
- I use appropriate language. ☐
- I design proper visual aids. ☐
- I rehearse out loud a minimum of three times. ☐
- I plan to pause. ☐
- I have a strategy to manage nerves. ☐
- I have prepared for questions. ☐

The horror story

Every so often I come across someone who has a presentation horror story. This is a time when they presented and it all went unspeakably wrong. I am talking worst case scenario, the scene we all dread, the silence we don't recover from, the going blank that breaks us.

Sometimes this experience is so traumatic it causes an individual to avoid presentations at all costs. They simply can't risk another failure, another humiliation, another public defeat.

If you are someone who has had such an experience I want you to think back to your horrible experience for me. I want you to be really honest and ask yourself why it went so wrong.

1. Were you told to speak at the last minute without any warning?
2. Were you not prepared enough but maybe didn't realise it until it was too late?
3. Did you realise too late your audience were not who you thought they were or your information was not relevant to them?
4. Did you have a catastrophic technology breakdown and were unable to deliver the talk without the slides?
5. Did you prepare in your head and then were unable to find the words?
6. Did your negative beliefs (nerves) gain control of your presentation leaving you paralysed with fear?

Any human being would fail in these circumstances because it was too late to deal with the situation they found themselves in. All of the above scenarios can be overcome with forward planning and preparation. One bad experience presenting does not need to dictate your presentation future.

I want you to chalk your negative experience up to just that, experience - something to learn from. The question is what did you learn?

What did you learn from your negative presentation experience?

If you haven't failed, you're not trying hard enough.

Chapter 11

Moving forward

After reading this book there are some actions I would like you to consider taking which I am going to explain in detail over the next few pages.

The actions are as follows:

- Work the three-step approach, use the checklists and get feedback.
- Prepare an action plan to up-skill.
- Implement the 12 × 12 plan to build the skill over the next year.

Work the approach, use the checklists and get feedback

Work the approach

The Presentation Book approach is:

1. Profile your audience
2. Structure and shape your messages
3. Design visual aids

The right approach
1. Profile your audience
2. Structure and shape your messages
3. Design visual aids

The first step is to commit to using this approach in preparing all your presentations going forward.

Use the checklist

I am terrified of flying in planes. I took a course to help me and what I learned on that course is that pilots and planes have back-ups for their back-ups.

Pilots go through a checklist before they take off and land. These could be pilots with years of experience flying but they still must go through the checklist every single time they take off and land. Why? Because forgetting even one tiny detail (which is so easily done) can have very serious consequences – life or death in the case of flying a plane.

Human memory just isn't reliable enough, especially if interrupted to briefly do something else, take a question someone has, or lend a hand momentarily. Once the mind has changed focus, all bets are off on memory.

It is for this reason I am giving a presentation checklist. I would like you to use it as a support in your presentation preparation. You are not to stand and present until you have ticked all the boxes.

I am also giving you a list of 'do's' and 'don'ts' as a quick reminder which you can put on your desk.

PLANNING THE CONTENT

I know what I want to happen as a result of the presentation.	
I have profiled my audience.	
The content is pitched at an appropriate level for my audience.	
I have kept to a maximum of three key points and supported them in a number of ways.	
My language is clear and simple to understand.	
I have found an interesting and attention-grabbing way to start.	
I have a strong ending to reinforce the messages.	
I have prepared for handling questions.	
I have created my handout and visuals separately.	

PLANNING FOR THE PRESENTER

I am confident about the knowledge and experience I have in this topic.	
I have checked the venue can supply all my technology needs.	
I am certain I know how to use the visual aids.	
I have rehearsed my presentation out loud a minimum of three times and have timed it.	
I have prepared clear and simple notes.	

PLANNING THE ROOM

There is a place for my laptop.	
There is a place to put my notes down.	
There are sockets for my equipment.	
I have a laser pointer if I need to point to something on the screen.	
I have water within reach.	
I have checked that my slides are visible from the back of the room.	

Get consistent feedback

Have you ever asked for feedback from a presentation only to be placated with some general statement like you were 'fine', 'yeah it was good'.

Or worse you are given critical feedback by a colleague: 'I think you were a bit nervous', 'You were talking very fast'.

Feedback is important because you need to understand the impact you are having on your audience. In order to get good feedback you need to ask a person in the audience to assess you based on specific criteria. You have to ask the right questions to get the right answers.

Opposite is a feedback sheet. You can give this to the person you're looking for feedback from and ask them to fill out.

Alternatively, there is one very simple question you can ask after your presentation to the person you are seeking feedback from. The question is: '*What messages did you take away from my presentation?*' Then wait and see what they say. No prompting from you allowed.

NAME	
Communication	
The presentation had a strong beginning.	
The presentation had key take-away messages.	
The presenter spoke in a language that was understandable.	
The presenter used examples/stories.	

Personal Impact	
The presenter used appropriate gestures.	
The presenter controlled their nerves.	
The presenter made eye contact and faced the audience at all times.	

Vocal Impact	
The presenter was audible.	
The presenter was passionate.	
The presenter spoke slowly and clearly.	

Presentation style: general observations	
The presenter spoke with authority and believability.	
The presenter was leading the slides.	
Notes	

Prepare an action plan

Action planning

You are not magically going to become a great presenter no matter how much you want it. You must take some action to move from where you are today to where you want to be.

If you want to be a better presenter, what you need to do is come up with specific actions you can take over the next 12 months to reach your goal. You may need to attend a course, get more experience presenting or read some more books.

You might want to try out Prezi, explore ways to get more energy or uncover ways to manage your nerves.

The actions are yours to determine. I have shared with you in this book what makes a great presenter so use that as your guide. Plan some specific actions you can take to get you to the next level as a presenter.

Use the presentation action plan below.

Three actions I can take within a month are:	1. 2. 3.
Three actions I can take within the next six months are:	1. 2. 3.
Three actions I can take within the next 12 months are:	1. 2. 3.

Implement the 12 × 12 plan

I said earlier in this book that one of the challenges some of you are facing is that you only present now and again.

- How can you build a skill when you don't get any practice?
- How can you learn from your mistakes if you don't get a chance to make any?
- How can you become a natural at something you never get to do?

The answer is you can't. Ah, but wait. You don't necessarily have to be formally presenting to build the skill. The components that make up a great presentation can be practised daily in your one-to-one interactions.

You are actually always presenting you just don't realise it. Every time you talk to someone face to face or on the phone you are presenting. Think about it. The only area you may not get to practise day to day is the use of visual aids but every other element you can practise in your everyday work situations.

The 12 × 12 plan means you select one behaviour a month for 12 months and wherever and whenever possible you put it into practice.

> **Ideally, try your new behaviour once a day for the month.**

These are the 12 behaviours I would like you to practise over the next 12 months.

12 × 12 plan

Month 1 Know what you want to achieve

Take a few seconds to think about what outcome you want from your everyday interactions. Afterwards ask yourself: Did I achieve it?

Month 2 Know your audience and where they are at

Take a minute to stand in the other person's shoes. How would you feel if you were them right now? Use the audience profile sheet once a day to prepare for an important conversation.

Month 3 Know your messages

Use the structure sheet once a day to prepare for an important conversation to get clear on what your messages are before you speak.

Month 4 Know how you will begin and end your communication

What's the first thing you will say? How are you going to wrap things up? Don't leave it to chance to prepare an opening and closing once a day.

Month 5 Have examples and analogies to support your messages

How can you make your everyday data more digestible? How can you engage everyone in your weekly staff meeting? Come with up a new example that will make your idea more understandable.

Month 6 Rehearse out loud three times before you do it for real

I am serious about this one. Before you head in to your boss to ask for an extra week's holiday, go into a room and speak it out loud three times to get clarity on your flow. It will work wonders.

Month 7 Plan to pause

Try to become as aware as possible of your speed of speech and plan to pause as much as possible in your everyday conversation.

Month 8 Have a strategy to deal with your nerves should they arise

What makes you nervous? What do your nerves look like? How can you build more confidence? Stop thinking about it and worrying about it and start doing something about it! Take a few minutes each day to focus on your breathing.

Month 9 Prepare for questions

Think about what questions the person you're talking to might have and how they might react to your information.

Month 10 Bring passion and energy to the room

It is so easy to slip into a mode of indifference in our everyday interactions. Become aware of your mood and your tone of voice. Smile. In person they can see it and on the phone they can hear it.

Month 11 Become aware of your body language

We rarely think about how we look and what we are doing with our hands on a daily basis. Bring some awareness to your movements. How do you sit? How do you stand? Are you someone who gestures or not?

Month 12 Review your skill

Over this final month I want you to examine what you have learned over the past 11 months. What behaviour did you find easy to do and what behaviour was uncomfortable for you? What worked and what didn't? When you got the result you wanted from your interactions was that down to chance or to your approach?

All for one and one for all – group presentations

A lot of you reading this book have to present as part of a group. The same rules apply to a group presentation as individual presentation. Below are some quick tips for group presentations.

Tips for group presentations

1. It's one presentation

A group presentation is one presentation with a number of presenters delivering it. It is not a number of different presentations coming together. It must be prepared, structured and delivered in a unified way.

2. **Consistency is key**

   The secret to success in a group presentation is consistency and flow. The message, structure, slides and group must appear and behave as one. All slides must look and feel the same. Agree the font, headings and graphics in advance of slide preparation.

3. **Choose a group leader**

   Choose a person from your group who will set the tone, introduce the talk, manage the Q&A, refer questions if necessary, take responsibility for managing any difficulties that may arise and make concluding remarks. The person you choose must be comfortable and confident doing this.

4. **Smooth transitions**

   One of the most challenging parts of a group presentation is transitioning from one presenter to the next. Each presenter must know how they will be introduced and how they will hand over to the next person. Ideally you want to summarise your talk and tell the audience how the next person will add to this. For example, 'Now that I have provided an overview of the market, Mary is going to show you how we intend to win you more business in this market.'

5. **How do I look**

   You must figure out how you will sit or stand as a group. Are you going to use a clicker or notes? Will you stand behind the podium or not? What are you wearing? All members must be dressed in suitable business attire.

6. **You are always on**

   In a group presentation even if you are not presenting you are still visible to the audience. Be aware of your body language and how you are sitting and standing. Don't slouch or appear bored or disinterested when others are speaking.

7. **Rehearse as a group**

   You must practise together out loud and be clear on who is saying what when. Also make sure you time the presentation. If you are presenting for five minutes then only present for five minutes.

8. Support each other

The presentation is being judged as a whole so you are only as good as your weakest link. Make sure everyone in the group is performing to the best of their ability. In answering questions make sure each person gets a chance to speak and contribute.

9. Mindful breathing

If you are the second or third speaker it can be a challenge to manage your nerves. You can calm your mind as you sit waiting to present by just observing the natural rhythm of the breath. You don't need to force it to be longer or slower. When your mind starts to wander and you are feeling very nervous just gently bring your attention back to the breath. You can count either 10 in-breaths or 10 out-breaths. If your mind wanders off mid-count just go back to the start.

10. Enjoy it!

Finally, I want to end the chapter by giving you a list of do's and don'ts as a quick reminder which you can put on your desk (see overleaf).

A one-pager for your desk

Top five tips for great presentations

1. **Know your material:** Before you can create understanding for your audience you must understand your own topic.
2. **Rehearse, rehearse, rehearse:** Practise what you are going to say out loud. You speak a presentation you don't write it. The spoken word and the written word are totally different.
3. **Know your audience:** Who are they? What do they know about your subject? What do they feel about it? What do you want them to be thinking and feeling after your talk?
4. **Know the room/equipment:** Check, double check and triple check everything.
5. **Breathe:** All the work should be done by the time you speak. Relax and breathe.

Top five biggest presentation blunders

1. **Starting with a whimper:** You need to start with a bang. You have 45 seconds to get their attention.
2. **Reading your presentation word for word:** A good speaker will always use notes to prompt them and keep them on track. A bad speaker will use PowerPoint as a crutch and read every slide.
3. **Failing to prepare:** An audience will always forgive you for being a little nervous but they will not forgive you for being unprepared.
4. **Not making it relevant:** What has your presentation got to do with your audience? What is the point?
5. **Speaking without passion:** If you are not interested in your subject how can anyone else be expected to be interested?

MY FINAL WORD

I attended a conference a few months ago and I told the group I was writing a book. At the break one of the guys came up to me and asked me about it. He said his wife was a coach and he thought she should write a book too, but his wife felt this would be too much of a slog for her. He asked me if this is how I felt about writing this book. I had never really thought about it until that moment. How did I feel writing this book? I was so busy writing I hadn't really stopped to think about my feelings until that moment.

Not for one single second has writing this book felt like a slog.

I wrote this book over many Sundays and a Christmas and it has been one of the most fun things I have ever done. I realise you think I am big loser now with no life but it really has been amazing to write this and I hope you have enjoyed reading it as much as I have enjoyed writing it. More than that I really hope, whoever you are, that you have taken something positive to help you on your professional development journey.

Thank you and good luck with all your future presentations.

APPENDIX: FULL WORKBOOK

Audience profiling template

Task 1	Who is in my audience for this presentation?
1.	
2.	
3.	

If there is a mixed audience in the room, who is the group I want to influence most? Is there a second or third group I wish to speak to?

Task 2	Before I present, what does my chosen audience know, think and feel about my presentation topic?
Know:	
Think:	
Feel:	

If my chosen audience members had *three questions* they wanted answered in my presentation, what would they be and in what order would they want them answered?

Task 3	After I finish my presentation what are the three messages I want my audience to take away and remember?
1.	
2.	
3.	

Structure template

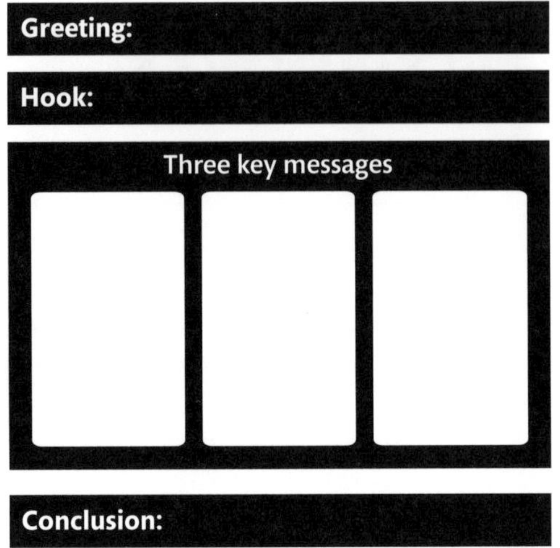

Slides template

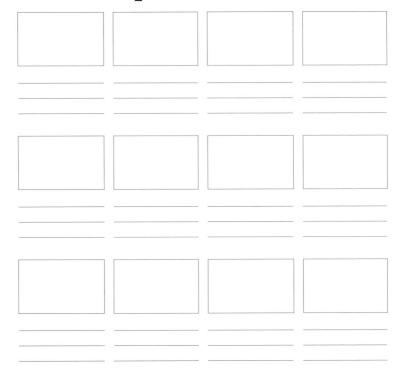

INDEX